FEEL GOOD 101

EMMA BLACKERY

sphere

SPHERE

First published in Great Britain in 2017 by Sphere

1 3 5 7 9 10 8 6 4 2

A CIP catalogue record for this book
is available from the British Library.

ISBN 978-0-7515-6923-0

Typeset in Dante by M Rules
Printed and bound in Great Britain by
Clays Ltd, St Ives plc

Papers used by Sphere are from well-managed forests
and other responsible sources.

Sphere
An imprint of
Little, Brown Book Group
Carmelite House
50 Victoria Embankment
London EC4Y 0DZ

An Hachette UK Company
www.hachette.co.uk

www.littlebrown.co.uk

DISCLAIMER
If you have any medical conditions or are not used to taking exercise, before undertaking
any of the exercises in this book or changing your exercise regime, please discuss this with
your GP or other medical practitioner. The information and opinions on healthy living and
well-being in the book are not intended to replace or conflict with the advice given to you
by your GP or other health professionals. The author and publisher disclaim any liability
directly or indirectly from the use of the material in this book by any person.

CONTENTS

Dead Trees

This book won't change your life. Let's just get that out of the way, shall we? Personally, I cannot stand walking into a bookshop and being bombarded by books with obnoxious bright red stickers on their covers that read, *Change your life today!* Or, *Join the millions of people who have revolutionised their lives with this book!* If you've ever picked up a book with those words on the front and actually bought the damn thing – you've been duped by a very clever marketing team. I'm sorry. (My publishers are probably already mad at me for writing that. Please publish my book.)

Right, good, so . . . are you sold yet? No? Here's the thing with books – they're just words on trees. Dead trees, to be exact. A tree died for this thing that you're holding (unless you're using an eReader, in which case, thank you for saving the trees. It's just a shame you look like an idiot holding one at the beach, isn't it?). Wait, is this also available on an eReader? Oh jeez. Sorry, publishers. (Please still publish my book.)

Back to my main point – a book alone cannot change your life. A therapist alone cannot change your life. A so-called 'life-changing moment' cannot change your life. The only entity that can actively shape your attitude and habits going forward is you. Yes, I'm aware of how clichéd that sounds, but reality hits hard – when it comes to turning your life around, you are the only person who can hit that *Big Red Button*. It is my hope that this book of which you're in possession can help you commit to the decisions you need to make in order to change your life for the better, but quite honestly, the ball is – and has always been – in your court. Most of your growth into a confident, happy human will come from inside of you, and will be born from the mistakes you make and lessons you learn along the way. Over many years, you will inevitably fuck up a numerous amount of times. You will make friends, lose friends, break hearts, have your own heart broken, feel shame, feel pride and, most of all, you will grow to love and accept yourself. Believe me, if I could tell my teenage self that I would be sitting here writing a sentence about self-acceptance at the age of twenty-five, I wouldn't have believed it. Take it from me – you don't need to buy this book to eventually find and love yourself (at this point, I'm pretty sure my publishers are crying). However: if you're able to take away just one thing from this book that gives you the confidence to make a decision that benefits your life, then I'm glad to have written it.

Just so you know (in case it isn't already extremely apparent), I'm not a therapist. I've had absolutely zero professional training in psychology or lessons in motivational speaking whatsoever. In fact, I genuinely had to Google the word 'preface' to make sure that it was the right one for this waffling introduction. I am merely an extremely outspoken born-on-the-Internet brat with a platform on which to speak my mind. I've been doing just that for over five years on YouTube – uploading usually short, mostly dumb videos to brighten someone else's day. Sometimes, just to shake things up a bit, I'll make a video with a little more 'purpose'; a message letting anybody and everybody know that the sadness they might feel at times is a sadness I have felt myself, and that it's normal, it's human – and most of all, temporary.

I'm not gonna try to tell you that you have to read this book in order to have an incredible life. You most certainly will, with or without my help – but if that's the case, why read it at all? Well, all I can say is that when I was younger, and felt as though I needed a voice of understanding and reason, I didn't have a *Feel Good 101*. I've lost friends, I've lost lovers, and at times I've lost hope altogether – but I am still here, in spite of it all. I've battled with depression and anxiety. I've experienced bullying and peer pressure. I've been the only child in a failed marriage. Needless to say, in my twenty-five years on this planet, I've been through the wars a little, and I have a lot to say about my experiences. It is my hope that the following pages can be a testament to human strength and perseverance – where there is despair, there is burning passion for a better life. Where there is a rock bottom, there is solid ground to build upon. Where there are dead trees, there is woody debris to support new growth. I am sitting here as an entirely different woman to the depressed, insecure girl I once was – hardened and battle-scarred, to be sure, but most importantly, I am happy, and I am hopeful. As you may well find out as you continue reading, I don't have much patience for false hope, empty promises or words of little substance, and so this is what I have to give: *Feel Good 101*. These are the lessons I have learned from my countless mistakes, and the most honest advice I could pluck from my brain and put down into words on thin slivers of dead trees. I truly believe with all of my heart and soul that this is the book I wish I had had growing up as the insecure, bullied, self-loathing doormat of a kid that I once was, filled with confusion, anger, fear and misery. Whilst it is my hope that you cannot relate to my story – if you can, then I wish for you that this book can sit as proof that unhappiness and hardship, whilst testing, is temporary, and that there is a wonderful world filled with love and opportunity waiting for you – you just have to press that *Big Red Button*.

I meant it when I said it, by the way: this book won't change your life – but you can. You are your own biggest limit in the world, but are also your own biggest hope. Only you can take the steps you need to help yourself become the strong, independent, fearless person you dream of being. However – it took me over twenty years of real lows, excruciating heartaches and countless mistakes to realise that I could take control of my own life. My hope in writing *Feel Good 101* is that it won't take you as long to realise this as it took me.

Now that it's written, I'm supposed to be professional and dedicate this book to someone, so here goes: To the person that held me back the most; to the person who told me every single day that I would never amount to anything – I'm glad you grew into the person I am today. Took you bloody long enough, didn't it?

TEN RULES FOR A HAPPIER LIFE

- Be a better person than you were yesterday.

- Always be the most honest person in the room.

- Apologise when something is your fault.

- Pride is a stronger feeling than hopelessness.

- Love without reservation.

- Be the person that is kindest to you.

- Nobody truly regrets following their heart.

- Say yes in spite of yourself.

- Smile in spite of yourself.

- Don't be a dick.

1

Chasing Your Dreams
(and not running out of breath)

'My Story'

Okay . . . book. Booky, booky, book book. I have to actually write a book. How do you write a book?! Perhaps I can Google it. Crap. When you're writing a preface, it sort of feels like you're just dicking around, you know? Oh shit, I've sworn already. Fuck, now I've *really* sworn. I said I wouldn't swear in Chapter One so that parents skimming through it wouldn't get mad and refuse to buy my book for their kids. Shit.

You know, there are probably some people reading this page and thinking, *Who is this girl, anyway? How did this even make it into a bookshop? Oh jeez, is she one of those 'YouTubers' that got lucky and now gets paid stupid money to talk to a camera?*

Okay, first of all, if that's what you believe, then congratulations, the tabloids have played you, just as they intended – sure,

I'm one of those 'YouTubers' *now*, and I *will* admit that it's easy to perceive me as 'lucky'. I'm not the funniest, prettiest or smartest kid on the Internet, so how did *I* land the chance to write a book when there are so many people out there who dream of their work being on the shelves? Listen, don't mistake me for someone who doesn't understand that point – I too have called myself 'lucky' many times throughout my life. In 2012, at the start of my tale, I was just a twenty-year-old punk equipped with only a few things: average school qualifications, a shitty 7 a.m.– 4 p.m. job in a café in a department store and a mental health issue that prevented me from flying the nest and becoming a person in my own right. I was miserable, being taken advantage of by my superiors at work, perceived as (and treated like) a doormat by the few friends I had in my life, and petrified at the thought of this being 'it' for ever – and it very nearly almost was.

So, skipping ahead a few years to the present day – how am I now here? How am I writing a book? How am I performing my music to crowds of thousands? How do I get to wake up when I want, say what I want, and make a living from it? I got lucky, right? Well ... yes and no. One could certainly argue that I was in the right place at the right time – but I wouldn't be where I am without both hard work and persistence. When most people I meet ask me to 'tell my story', my instinct is to roll my eyes so hard that my retinas detach. I get that my YouTube 'story' is relatively new and interesting to those not in the know, but how can anyone be expected to summarise a twenty-five-year journey from hardship to happiness in a few short sentences?

With all that said, here it is: the full story of how my YouTube career began, all the way back in 2012, and, if nothing else, at least now when someone asks how I 'became a YouTuber', I can just say, 'Well, buy my book. It's in Chapter One.'

3.58 p.m. I lift the metal container of baked beans from the bain-marie and away from the serving area entirely, out of any customer's sight. *No one is going to order a jacket potato at this time in the afternoon*, I say to myself. *They're probably getting too cold to serve anyway.*

3.59 p.m. I reach around to grip the strings of my uniform apron and pull them loose. I breathe a sigh of relief as another shift at the department store café draws to a close, scrunching up my apron and clutching it tightly, as though it were a stress ball. It got covered in flour again today. *If I turn up with it in this state tomorrow, I'll be pulled into the office – again. Better wash it when I get home.*

4 p.m. I quickly look around the café, scanning the scene for my supervisor, Jessica. The coast is clear. I pick up my pace, making my way out of the café and on to the shop floor of the department store. I dash past rails of clothing and towards the giant escalator in the middle of the shop floor. As I place one foot on to the metal steps and proceed upwards to the staff room on the upper floor, I see Jessica, making her way down on the opposite escalator towards the café.

'Oh, is it four o'clock already?' she says as we pass each other. 'Come back down to the café, I'll need to check to see how clean the kitchen is. You know you can't leave until it's spotless.' I close my eyes, trying to stifle a sigh – there are two other members of staff still on duty for the next two hours in the café that could have tidied any mess I had left in the kitchen. I place my apron over my head and tighten the strings.

4.01 p.m. We step back into the kitchen. Jessica shakes her head. 'Really? You call this work surface "clean"?' She sighs. Give it another wipe-down and then you can go, I suppose.' With a frustrated, audible grunt, I swipe a cloth from the store cupboard, coat it in cleaning detergent and wipe down the surface, all under Jessica's watchful eye.

4.04 p.m. As per Jessica's instruction, four minutes after my shift was supposed to be over, I proceed to walk over to the café tables and wipe them clean, too. I start to wonder if my dad is calling me on my phone, which is up in my locker in the staff room. He always tells me I need to stand up for myself; that at 4 p.m., I'm no longer obligated to stay, and that I can't get in trouble for just saying 'no' and signing out on time. Watching my other on-duty colleagues chatting at the tills, I imagine myself finally snapping at Jessica, telling her to 'shove it' and simply walking out. I then imagine walking into the store the next morning, being led upstairs to face an 'internal investigation' by the store manager and being fired. My heart begins to race as I imagine the prospect of applying for a new job and being asked, 'So, why did you leave your last job?' and having to tell them I was fired for storming out. I continue wiping tables.

4.20 p.m. I am filling the refrigerator with sandwiches for the next morning. Jessica walks over in a strop. 'Okay, go on, you can leave,' she huffs. I walk past the counter, once again scrunching up my apron in my hand. 'Oh, excuse me!' calls out an elderly customer who had crept up behind me. 'May I please have a jacket potato with baked beans?'

4.35 p.m. I finally drag my bag out of my locker in the staff room, slamming the locker shut in frustration. I read the text from my dad that accompanies my missed calls: *Where are you?*

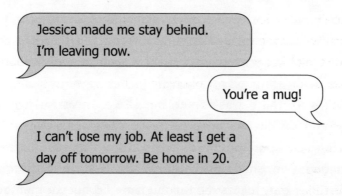

Jessica made me stay behind. I'm leaving now.

You're a mug!

I can't lose my job. At least I get a day off tomorrow. Be home in 20.

I put on my coat, walk down the corridor and out on to the shop floor. I catch Jessica walking towards the staff room I have just come out of, paperwork in her hand. 'Oh, by the way,' she says with an air of superiority, 'Janet phoned earlier, she's not going to be coming in tomorrow. Are you all right to start at 7 a.m. tomorrow?'

I sigh. 'Yes, of course. See you tomorrow.'

*

Now, I have no doubt that this story is nothing new to those who have worked a nine to five, nor will it probably seem bad in comparison to stories that many of you out there may have – however, as those who have done it will also tell you, it is difficult to be content with your life when this is basically all it contains: *waking up to go to work, being bossed around, eating dinner, going to sleep, repeat.* At the age of twenty, I had been in my waitressing/ kitchen job for two years, with no perceivable future prospects, no chance of promotion, and no time or qualifications to help me get a better job. I was well and truly stuck in the rat race, squeaking and dragging my tail six, sometimes seven, days a week. This job was supposed to fill up an uneventful gap year – one I had taken because I was completely petrified of leaving my home town and leaving my dad all alone in order to attend university, and I think I knew deep down that I was never going to actually go. So that was it: I was a waitress.

Oh, well, there was something else – I was a singer in a band, too, on the rare occasion that I was given a day off from serving jacket potatoes to old ladies. It was the one escape I had from being smushed under Jessica's big, bossy, supervisor feet day in, day out. It was the second time I'd been a member of a band, and it would turn out to be the last. I'd applied to fill the position of *vocalist* when the band's previous singer quit in order to go on a TV talent show. It was the band's drummer who had got me in to replace her. We only did small, local gigs, but boy, was I committed – when our guitarist allowed anyone else to have even a smidgen of input with the songwriting, I was bringing sheets of my own lyrics to rehearsals, dreaming of the day we'd break out of the county of Essex and play a show in an unfamiliar city. On one occasion, we actually did land a gig out of town; however, on the way to the show in Brighton, we got caught in a ten-car pile-up on the motorway, totalling our rental van (along with a classic car that was worth more than any of us had ever earned in our lives). Nevertheless, with determination, willpower and an engine leaking anti-freeze, we somehow made it to our show. I got a tattoo of a van with smoke pouring from the bonnet as a memento. This band was my future, I was sure of it: yes, I had some demos of some solo work, but I knew that one day my band would make it big, and I could leave my waitressing job, rude elderly customers and jacket potatoes behind for ever.

And then I got kicked out.

It probably shouldn't have been a shock, really. After at least six concurrent weeks of at least one band member not being able to make rehearsals, our guitarist (I shall refrain from airing my personal feelings towards him here) decided we should 'take a break'. Naively, I wholeheartedly agreed – it would give me the chance to book some time off work, write some new lyrics and come back refreshed and ready to take on the world – right? Imagine the look on my face a few weeks later when I checked Twitter one morning and saw a post from the band's account that went something along the lines of: *We're finally back! Come see us play our first reunion show with our original line-up! Buy your tickets here . . .*

No one had told me. No one from my band, which I had loved so much that I had gotten a tattoo of our totalled van on my leg, had given me the courtesy of a call or even a text to tell me that they'd 're-formed' with their previous singer. I'd been publicly

kicked out in the most humiliating way. That same day, after
many angry tears, I marched down to a local tattoo studio and got
a design that covered up the tattoo on my leg, feeling devastated
that the people that I considered my closest friends could hurt me
in such a callous way.

I knew almost immediately that I wasn't done with music. I didn't
know what I was going to do, or how I was going to do it, but I was
going to keep writing and releasing songs. Before I'd joined my
band, I'd created a YouTube channel for my solo music that went
under the name *TheseSilentSeas* (pretentious, sure, but I thought it
was artsy and *cool*) where I'd uploaded some acoustic demos that
I'd recorded in my bedroom with some free music software. Could
I go back to that channel and go back to writing under that name,
as though the band and its subsequent drama had never happened?
No – I was going to go solo. *Officially* solo. Over the following
weeks, I compiled the acoustic demos I had recorded into my first
ever EP, titled *Human Behaviour*, put them online for purchase under
my real name for the very first time, and opened a brand-new
YouTube channel just to claim the username: emmablackery.

As I began to upload my home-made demos to my brand-new
channel, I realised that in order to achieve my dream of becoming a successful solo artist, I would need to dedicate as much
time to YouTube as I could. Whenever I was given a rare day
off work, I would sit in my bedroom, write brand-new songs on
my acoustic guitar and record them with a cheap microphone.
I would then proceed to spam my own Facebook wall with my
new creations in a desperate attempt to get anyone and everyone
I knew to give my songs a listen. I began to upload covers of popular songs and even started making content that wasn't strictly

music-related, such as Q&A videos, in the hope of gaining a new audience. One evening, after searching YouTube for ideas for new and exciting content, I accidentally stumbled across the underground world of vlogging. I'd certainly seen kids talking to their webcams in the past, and had even attempted it myself once or twice, but hadn't given it too much thought. Yet, here in front of me were people my age, talking into professional cameras with *hundreds of thousands* of viewers tuning in to hear what they had to say! It was that night back in May 2012 when I realised what I wanted to do. I was going to build an audience of my own by sharing my life online, in the hope of perhaps one day being able to quit my job at the café and becoming a full-time musician like I'd always dreamed.

After a few nights of planning, I decided that if I truly wanted to build up a YouTube channel, I had to get a decent camera. I began to research what equipment my new YouTube heroes had, and discovered that DSLRs were the new thing that 'vloggers' were using; suddenly, videos in beautiful HD quality were popping up all over the site! However, when I decided to do a quick Google search for the specific camera my favourite vlogger was using, after pausing their video in the right spot, my heart sank. The cheapest one I could find was just over £630. My monthly wage at the department store café varied between £600 and £800! The only way I could possibly afford one (and still afford to live) was to put the DSLR on a credit card. *This is a stupid idea*, I said to myself, hesitantly entering my card details. *You won't be able to pay this off for years, and you'll only use it once for a crappy music video, and then give up. This is stupid. Don't do it.*

I did it anyway.

I pressed the *complete transaction* button and sat back in my desk chair. Had I really just blown £630 that I couldn't afford on a DSLR camera? I had zero expertise on how to use one – I'd never even held one before! I was utterly clueless, and suddenly very worried about what I had just gotten myself into. What kind of judgement would I get from my friends and family when they found out I'd blown a month's wages on a camera that I would definitely give up on using after one try?!

When the postman arrived a few days later with my new purchase, I ran to the front door and eagerly unwrapped it. The camera was heavy, bulky and definitely more complicated than the crappy handheld I'd been using previously – I instantly sensed I was out of my depth. The next few evenings were spent at my laptop, furiously researching anything to do with DSLRs. What did 'aperture' mean? What was 'shutter speed'? Couldn't I just turn it on, press record, and get a beautiful music video? My question was answered as soon as I came home from the local park after filming my first home-made music video for my song, 'Fixation'. No, you most *definitely* couldn't just press record and get a masterpiece. My attempt at a music video was laughable, even by my 2012 standards (or lack thereof). I didn't manage to film enough footage before my tiny memory card ran out of space, so I had to copy and paste one of the scenes three different times (I even played the scene in reverse at one point to make it look like a different take – 2012 Emma had a lot of balls, and zero dignity). Most of the footage was also grainy and out of focus! Was this all a DSLR could do?

With a sigh, I uploaded my haphazard attempt at a video, hoping the music itself would bring in the views from my three(!)

subscribers, and sadly put my new toy aside. What a waste of money.

A couple of months passed. By day, during time off from my job, I'd pick up my DSLR again, spurt some rubbish about my life into the camera and upload it, hoping that something I said would go viral and that new people would find my music video. By night, I would watch my favourite YouTubers – including a guy who would read a popular (but poorly written) young-adult novel out loud to his camera and give his comedic opinion on it. YouTube, despite not feeling like something I could do very well myself, quickly became my new escape. When I was watching videos from my favourite vloggers, I wouldn't be thinking about Jessica bossing me about at work, or the £630 on my credit card that I couldn't pay off. I wouldn't be thinking about the fact that I had no future plans, no traditional career ambition, no desire to leave home due to my specific type of anxiety – I was simply laughing at YouTubers talking about procrastination, or about things they'd thought were true when they were kids, or slightly weirder videos of vloggers painting their entire body in purple paint. There was always something new, with the ability to distract me from a bad day at work, and the videos were always from someone I felt was truly talking to and connecting with *me*. These guys *got me*. I still remember the evening I sat at my computer, watching the latest episode of the young-adult novel being ripped apart, and thinking to myself, *Didn't that* Fifty Shades of Grey *book just come out? Isn't that supposedly quite cringey? What if instead of talking about music . . . I try reading that and criticising it?* To my surprise, I found the jump from making music-based vlogs to comedy videos a lot easier than I'd imagined. After many years of being teased at school, I'd quickly turned to humour to hide my insecurities, and I'd always thought my wit was a strength – even though I'd never considered it as a career option. The first episode of my 'Let's Read: *Fifty Shades of Grey*' series was uploaded in June 2012. Whilst I was nervous and unnatural on camera, and the video was poorly lit and terribly edited with some free software I found on my laptop, I wholeheartedly believed that I was making content that the world would enjoy. In time, I'd be proven right.

Between the months of July and December in 2012, my life changed dramatically. My 'Let's Read: *Fifty Shades of Grey*' series was taking off (the first video in the series reached over 100,000 views, which in 2012 was no mean feat). I'd begun uploading comedy vlogs and sketches of my own, and I'd somehow plucked up the courage to request more days off work and was spending them looking for a job with less demanding hours. I subsequently found one, as a manager in a new café in town, which meant fewer hours and slightly more money. I was happy – but of course, what goes up . . .

One evening in late December 2012, I logged in to YouTube, and was faced with something I'd never seen before. In front of me was a bright pink alert on my homepage:

ATTENTION. We have received copyright complaint(s) regarding material you posted, as follows: 'Let's Read: Fifty Shades of Grey*': Episode 2.*

Please note: Repeat incidents of copyright infringement will result in the deletion of your account and all videos you have uploaded. Please delete any videos for which you do not own the necessary rights, and refrain from uploading infringing videos.

Well, needless to say, I was scared shitless. My heart started to pound. It turned out that someone at the publishing house for *Fifty Shades of Grey* had seen my series and put in a copyright notification to get my series of critiques taken down. If I'd known then what I know now, I would have fought back. I would've claimed the commentary and criticism made the original work transformative and that it had every right to exist, but alas, I was young and new to the platform – and so I deleted every video in the 'Let's Read' series. *Every. Single. One.* Oh, how I wish I'd backed up my content to a hard drive – sadly, I can find no backup copies of any of the twenty-two videos I made for the series, and I have long since accepted that they are gone for ever. Looking back, however, I see this terrifying, pink-tinted warning as a blessing in disguise. It was from this copyright takedown that I decided to finally bite the bullet and press on with my original comedy sketches and vlogs. My first real 'comedy vlog' was called '*Zelda of GTFO*', where I talked about how any future partner of mine would need to love *The Legend of Zelda* game series as much as I do. It was, of course, these types of videos that then became more popular than my 'Let's Read' series ever was, and helped to grow my channel to numbers I'd never even dreamed of having just months previously. By December 2012, just seven months after starting my channel, I'd reached 20,000 subscribers.

And then . . . I got fired from my managerial job. Yep! I was pulled aside after a shift at the new café on Christmas Eve and told that, as a manager who only came in for four-hour shifts, I was of little value to the company and was being let go. However, when a window closes, sometimes, a big-ass door opens. I left the café that night without a single tear rolling down my face – YouTube had become such a passion project of mine that despite earning only a fraction of what my 'real job' was giving me, I'd been pouring every hour I could into the site. Towards the end of my time there, I was coming up with new ideas at work and writing scripts for them instead of serving customers, walking around the back out of sight to check my views, using every day off as an opportunity to film new videos and editing them in the evenings after work until the early hours, resulting in me getting into work the next day absolutely exhausted. Needless to say, I was a sucky manager, and by all rights, I probably deserved to be fired. However, despite concern from my dad about my income (and now a gap in employment on my CV) I knew that this was a sign. This was my time – and I had to give it everything I had.

That evening, I told my dad I'd been let go, and said to him, 'Dad, you need to trust me. I can make a living from this. Maybe one day I'll actually earn more from YouTube than I did at the café. I have to take this opportunity and see what happens.'

I would say that my dad was supportive from the get-go, but I wouldn't want to lie in my own book. He was concerned that one month I'd do well with YouTube earnings, and the next month earn nothing at all. I think, looking back, that if I hadn't been so caught up in my new passion I probably would have agreed with him, but by the time my last shift rolled around on New Year's Eve, I was in too deep. YouTube was going to be my future – no more early starts, no more workplace bullying, no more worrying about what I wanted to do for a living: this was the answer.

Since early 2013, YouTube has been my full-time job, my passion, my livelihood, and the rest of my story is visible for the world to see through my hundreds of videos. In the few months after being fired, I would begin to upload comedy sketches on a weekly basis, reach the 100,000 subscriber milestone, make videos with creators I looked up to, return to music and release a second solo EP that would reach number one in the iTunes Rock Chart in the UK. To date, I have completed my first ever headline tour (which sold out in minutes), supported Busted in arenas across the country, reached one million subscribers (and counting!), overcome enough of my anxiety issues to move out of my dad's house and live on my own, communicated my message of determination and the importance of hard work to millions of people across the world, headlined Shepherd's Bush Empire in London and now I've written a book.

Oh, and in case you were wondering: I paid off that credit card, too.

Luck Is For Losers

So, you were a waitress, and you happened to catch a break, you're thinking. It could've happened to anyone. Let me tell you – I've thought the exact same. I've lost count of the amount of times I've called myself 'a waitress that got a chance'. The thing is – and this is something that I understand can be hard to appreciate when it isn't directly visible – it's taken a lot of hard work for me to get to where I am now. Listen, I'm in no position to complain. I love what I do. I wake up every morning in disbelief that I can actually call what I do my job. However, it has involved years of consistent creative thinking, filming, editing, uploading, posting on social media, keeping up with trends, doing research, flying across the world at all hours to be at events – it is a wonderful life, but definitely an exhausting one, and not one I could uphold without a lot of dedication. I realise now that yes, having my videos gain a bit of traction at the beginning may have been a stroke of luck, buried somewhere deep in an algorithm that no one understands, but those *Fifty Shades* videos providing entertaining critique that no one on Youtube was providing, and maintaining and building my audience would not have been possible without a lot of grafting – ultimately, my videos would not have taken off if I hadn't worked to make them the best that I could.

My first videos in 2012 were certainly not incredible, but improvement comes from practice: watching each and every video from those who influenced me, learning their editing techniques, researching lenses and microphones to make my videos the best quality I could afford. My point is, if you want results, you have to put in the work. So did I get lucky to begin with, or did I just provide the content that was missing at the time? Perhaps both statements are correct, but it's important to remember that luck alone gets you nowhere. One of my heroes, ex-wrestler and MMA fighter CM Punk, once said that luck is for losers. Straight and to the point, but when you think about it, quite true. At the end of the day, you have to make your own luck – waiting around for a dream to happen will get you nowhere. Believe me – I know a lot about that, too.

Let me tell you a story. When I was growing up, an only child in my home town of Basildon, Essex, I listened to the music you'd expect a girl from the early '90s to like – Spice Girls, S Club 7, Steps, Britney Spears, and basically any pop song from one of those big compilation CDs that my dad would rent from our local library. Ever since I learned to talk at the age of three (I was a late developer . . . I'm still waiting to reach adult height, too), I loved singing. I dreamt of being the lead singer in a pop group, sketching rubbish pictures every day after school of myself on stage with my friends. When my parents got me listening to '80s icons such as Michael Jackson and Madonna, I began to dream of being a solo artist instead. As soon as I was old enough to be able to use a Walkman, I developed a habit of listening to my favourite songs in the dark when I was supposed to be asleep, pretending my pitch-black bedroom was a stage, in front of me a sea of lights from a screaming crowd watching me perform. I'm not ashamed to admit this habit actually continued long into my twenties. (Do I still do it? I'm not telling you.)

Sadly, when I was growing up, our family never had much money to spare. I'm not going to sit here and say we were dirt poor – we paid our bills, we never went without food and we always had a roof over our heads – but things were tight enough to mean that asking my parents if I could go to a stage school or take singing lessons was out of the question. I don't even recall ever asking them, as I knew what the answer would be. It wasn't that my parents didn't want to support me – I guess they just saw my singing as a nice hobby, and that putting money behind something that wouldn't be a full-time job would be a waste of money that could go on other things. I don't blame them for that, nor do I wonder, *What if I'd gone to theatre school?* I know that we simply did what was smart, and what was best for our family. However, when I was twelve (and posters of bands such as Busted, McFly and Green Day had begun to take over my bedroom walls), my dad took me into our local music store and allowed me to pick out an early birthday present.

My first guitar, I'm not ashamed to say, was a piece of shit (sorry, Dad). It was an electric guitar with a snakeskin pattern, equipped with a bright yellow strap that read, *POLICE LINE – DO NOT CROSS.* Paired with my £20 portable amp, I felt like the coolest up-and-coming musician of my generation. I, my friends, was hot shit. Trying hard to learn how to play the simplest of riffs on one string (hello, 'Seven Nation Army') and not realising that when strings went rusty they needed changing; not understanding what bass, middle and treble were on my amp, and thus turning all three dials up to maximum – I was a rock GODDESS. To be honest, I didn't even really play the damn thing, or learn any songs the whole way through – most of the time I just stood in my bedroom, unplugged guitar around my body, jumping in the air in time to a chorus, dreaming of the day I'd be appointed as the fourth member of Busted. A pipe dream, sure, but one I acted out on my own every afternoon after school. Someday, I'd be sharing a stage with Busted. I think that, in my head, I knew it was rubbish – I wasn't in a band, I wasn't writing my own music, I didn't even know anything about the music industry – I just had a dream, something that would distract me from the usual suspects: homework, body issues, bullying and every other distraction that came with growing up.

After a couple of years of occasionally picking up my snakeskin axe and frustratingly putting it back down when I couldn't nail a certain chord change, I did the only thing I knew – I gave up entirely. Giving up is one of the easiest things to do, and it's something I've ashamedly done many times with different things over the years – violin, crochet, wrestling training, karate, personal training, healthy eating, about five different YouTube channels . . . the list is endless – but on this occasion, as far as music went, I well and truly wrote myself off. I still practised singing, pretending to be in a band when the bedroom lights were out, but by the age of fourteen, as my guitar began to gather dust and

Busted announced they were splitting up, I left my dreams in the corner, throwing myself into academic subjects instead. The thing is, surrounded by my peers at school who knew exactly what they wanted to do for a living, I was completely lost. Being a singer was the only real 'dream' I'd ever had, the only career I could imagine doing that made me smile at the prospect. Without that dream, all I could do was drift, not knowing what else I'd be any good at: *Perhaps I should become an English teacher, or a secretary like my mum. Not that I'll be doing either, if I keep skipping homework . . .*

It wasn't until I'd turned sixteen, after a spur-of-the-moment decision to buy an acoustic guitar with my saved-up pocket money, that my love for playing music truly came back. This time around, I was older and knew myself a little better, equipped with more acoustic-based music influences, and I began to write full-length songs for the first time. I shared my creations with no one; after coming this far, I was terrified of negative feedback, scared of having anything knock my confidence and send my new guitar into its dusty grave alongside its predecessor. Slowly, with practice, I got better at playing; I got the hang of singing and strumming at the same time, and of writing lyrics that fitted into my personal life.

Now fully immersed in the world of pop-punk bands such as Paramore, blink-182 and Green Day, I finished school and attended college to study A levels in academic subjects. I still wasn't convinced that I could eventually sell out shows with what little music I'd created, and made the decision to turn down a course in music production, instead opting to study maths, ICT, English language and politics (could you imagine me debating in a politics class? I was every bit as annoying as you'd think). Within the first couple of weeks, I'd befriended a guy in my politics class whose love for bands such as Nine Inch Nails and Rage Against The Machine rubbed off on me. However, it was only when he introduced me to a band called Placebo that I realised I had to truly give music another go. I had to give myself as much of a chance as I could to share a stage with Placebo one day, just as I'd once dreamed of doing with Busted.

In 2010, after discovering my new desire to be in a band, another college friend suggested a website where existing bands were advertising for members. One night when I was eighteen, after I came home from studying, I logged on, typed in my location, and up came an advert: *Southend-based band looking for male vocalist to make pop-punk music like Four Year Strong, Paramore, The Wonder Years. 16–22 age range. Email here for more details . . .*

I stared long and hard at the ad. It'd been on the site for weeks – had the band already found someone and just not removed their post? *Besides, they're looking for a* male *vocalist,* I thought to myself. *I'd look like a fool applying. Although, they* did *say they wanted to make music like Paramore . . . and I do love Paramore . . .*

. . . Ah, screw it. Just apply. They can only say no, right?

Heart thumping in my chest, I wrote to the email address in the ad. *I don't have any real band experience,* I wrote, already tasting the rejection before I could even hit send. *And I know I'm female, but I'd love to send over some vocals if you'd consider me.*

Before long, I had an email back: *Hey Emma. Sure thing, send over a sample of you singing something. Do you know 'Wasting Time' by Four Year Strong? Send over a take of you singing that.*

Crap. I didn't know that song. I quickly typed in the band's name on Spotify and up came the song he'd requested. *Oh man, this is heavier than Paramore. And the guy's got a strong, screamy voice,* I thought to myself. *You're going to sound awful attempting this.*

Although – I'd come *this* far, right? I grabbed my cheap USB microphone, plugged in some headphones and (nervously) sang over the track. Attaching the demo, I sent my reply to the guitarist: *Okay, here you go. It's not really my style, but I gave it a shot. If you want, I could probably sing a Paramore song instead – might be better!*

After what felt like an eternity (yet was only a few, short minutes) I received a reply: *This is cool! Wanna come and have a jam this weekend?*

My heart soared. I was in a band! That Saturday morning, I phoned in sick at my then-job at a fast food restaurant and went to Southend for my first ever band practice. The band, who we'll refer to as BBD, made me feel as though, for the first time in my life, my bedroom pipe dreams could become a reality. Just a week after joining, we played our first gig: a three-song set in the middle of a shopping centre for a local Battle of the Bands competition. Okay, so we didn't win the competition (mostly because I was nervous as heck, apparently not a good singer when performing in front of a crowd and couldn't remember any of the lyrics!), nor did we win the *next* Battle of the Bands a few months later, either – but the gigs we played to the ten, sometimes fifteen people at local venues were a dream. Up on stage, singing into a microphone as I stood at the monitors in front of me – I felt at home. I felt as though I had truly found my purpose.

Then something bad happened. Don't date your band members. I'll summarise – I started dating the bassist; the guitarist (the one I sent the demo track to) was none too happy. BBD pretty much went downhill from there, and ended over a few short Facebook messages, just a few short months after I'd joined. The bassist and I stayed together for about three months after the band broke up, but our relationship fizzled out. However, the arguments we had that led to us breaking up left me reeling, and I decided I needed to vent in the only way I knew how – I wrote a song.

On 1 September 2011, after ambushing my bassist-turned-boyfriend-turned-ex at a tattoo parlour, where he was getting his first tattoo, I returned home, smug at 'getting revenge' on a guy who had broken my heart. I sat down at my desk, wrote a song called 'Glory Days (I Hate You More)', switched on my crappy handheld camera and recorded myself performing it. *Okay, now I just need to upload it so he'll see it*, I thought to myself (I'm really painting myself as a bad ex here, aren't I? I swear I've matured), as I created a channel. I went with the name TheseSilentSeas and uploaded the video. It was the first song I'd written outside of a band that I was truly proud of. My bassist-turned-boyfriend-turned-ex wrote a song in retaliation (which, let's be real, dude, sucked) and that was that. I was now *TheseSilentSeas*, solo musician. By this point, I had left college and had been working in the department store café for a year, using what little free time I had to write more music, spurred on by my 120 views on 'Glory Days'. It was through a mutual friend that I met the guy who would produce my first solo EP, *Human Behaviour*, who then invited me to join the band that he played drums for – and now you're up to date. Joined the new band, got kicked out, got mad, went solo under my real name, started the channel emmablackery, started messing around with comedy videos, and the rest, as they say, is history.

In mid-2013, a year after starting the emmablackery channel and cementing myself as a YouTube personality, I went back into the studio, recording and self-releasing my second EP *Distance*. Within the first week, the music video for the lead single 'Go The Distance' had reached hundreds of thousands of views, the EP was number one on the iTunes Rock Chart, and big record labels were coming from out of nowhere asking for meetings. I began performing acoustic shows at YouTube events, joining my fellow 'YouTube musicians' on tour, and released my third solo EP, *Perfect*, in late 2014. After a performance at Summer in the City later that year, where I sang tracks from my EP and shaved my head for charity in front of thousands of people, I signed with management for the first time, releasing my fourth EP *Sucks To Be You* in early 2016. Just before the EP's release, I received a bit of inside gossip – Busted, my favourite band as a kid, the band that inspired me to pick up a guitar in the first place, were re-forming and going on a nationwide arena tour . . . and they were inviting me to be the support act to open for each and every show.

At twelve years old, I picked up my first guitar, looking up at the walls of Busted posters in my bedroom, dreaming of an alternative universe where I would befriend them and play a show with them to crowds of thousands.

At twenty-four, I did just that, at Wembley Arena.

All right, that was a long story, well done on sticking with me. Go and have a drink, or something. I didn't achieve my dream the way that I'd imagined as a kid, I suppose – you know, signing with an agent from a young age, sending demos to each and every record label, having every little thing about my image changed – I got here my way. I did the grafting – I taught myself guitar, having never been taught by anyone else. I sought out local bands to play with. I played those gigs in grotty bars to fewer than ten people. I wrote and recorded those demo songs, I released those EPs, and I made those hundreds of videos, both music and comedy. I played those events and went on those tours. From the second I decided I wanted to take being a musician seriously, I worked my arse off to get what I wanted. You see, there is no 'right' or 'wrong' way to get to where you want – just *your* way. Luck is for losers. Work for what you want, and never give up on that dream in the back of your mind. Perhaps the dream you have for yourself right now won't work out – but if you at least try, there's a chance you'll succeed. If you don't try at all, there's zero chance you'll succeed. So why not give it your all?

Whose Life Is It, Anyway?

In 2002, at the age of ten, I borrowed my dad's big, bulky camcorder from the '90s and set it up on a tripod in my bedroom. What can I say? I was destined to be a vlogger. I pressed record, ran over to my CD player, and played the track 'I Will Always Love You' by Whitney Houston. A classic, might I add, if sung well, and not in a bar on karaoke night when drunk. I have since made that mistake.

After belting out the lyrics over the top of the track, I pressed stop on the camcorder and ran downstairs to grab my dad.

'Daddy! Come and look! I sang "I Will Always Love You"!' I said excitedly, running over to the man resting on the sofa, tugging on his arm.

'I heard, darling,' he replied. 'I think the whole street heard you. You have the voice of an angel . . . '

I beamed.

'. . . an angel chewing on broken glass.'

As his joke sank in, I laughed along with him, trying to hide my tears. Listen, my dad was very supportive overall – I am in no way trying to suggest otherwise. There was a time when I sang 'Tragedy' on holiday in Gran Canaria and my dad recorded the entire thing and proceeded to play it proudly on his computer every night for the next year. But this joke . . . it hurt. All right, it was a *joke*, but to me, it felt as though there was a layer of truth hiding underneath – did he really think I sounded bad? *Did* I sound bad? Did he just want me to shut up for the night?

Needless to say, there were times growing up when it seemed as though my parents were trying desperately to keep me humble – I certainly wasn't a child prodigy like you see on TV shows, but there were times when my mum would be too tired from working in London all day to really pay attention to my passion, and the little jokes here and there from my dad stung more than I let on. With a little help from our good friend *hindsight*, I can see now that really, though it may have been hurtful being made to believe in myself way more than anyone else did – it was the best thing my parents could have done. Could you imagine if they'd told me every single day that I was the best singer in the world, when looking back, I *so* clearly wasn't? Would I have taken rejection from future Battle of the Bands auditions so kindly? What kind of person would I have become?

Sadly, my growing self-doubt over my singing ability affected me long into my teens. Instead of belting out my favourite songs,

I began to mumble them instead, only truly practising when I was home alone. Our family had very little money to spare, as I mentioned previously, but my lack of confidence was another reason I never asked my parents if I could go to theatre school, or to get singing lessons – they didn't seem to think I could make a living from my singing voice, so why should I even try?

At sixteen, when it came to choosing courses to study at college, I scanned over the prospectus to consider my options. Amongst courses in French, mathematics, English language, all of which I excelled at in school – another type of course stood out. Music production – a course that would last two years and consisted purely of analysing popular songs, working out *why* they were considered good, and learning how to replicate that sound in the studio. To someone who had started to write their own songs on acoustic guitar just a couple of years before, this course seemed like a dream – I could learn how to record my own music, and then I could send demo CDs out to labels, get signed and become the next big thing!

I had a real opportunity to chase my dream – so naturally, I chose to take mathematics, English language, politics and ICT instead. Academic subjects were *safer*, and would get me a fairly decent job or place at a university – even though I had zero desire to work in an office or go to university. Being on a stage performing was still the only career I could envision for myself. In the same way that my friends wanted to go into law, or business, I wanted to sing – anything else wouldn't have compared. Still, I stuck with what I knew I would be good at by taking subjects that would be looked at favourably on a CV. My parents have always said to me that this is *my* life, and that

I can choose to do whatever I want with it – but still I didn't even mention the music production course to them. I felt that even though they had both always insisted that I was entitled to make my own destiny, they would still secretly think that I was throwing my life away, wasting my education on something I'd never use. Perhaps they wouldn't have done, but I wasn't going to risk disappointing them – I'd done well in school, and I knew I'd do well in college, too.

Only, I didn't do so well. I mean, I did okay in the subject I liked, which was English language – but still, you can spell ACDC with my results (which is actually quite cool, if you ask me). I just couldn't apply myself, constantly distracted in class by friends, skipping homework and coursework deadlines to perform with my first band – because my heart wasn't in anything else. I knew by the start of my second year in college that I didn't want to go through another step of education, and thus made the decision to take a gap year and figure out what I could do, if music wasn't going to be my future. I quit my part-time job as a fast food worker at the end of college and went into my department store waitressing job, where I stayed for another two years.

So there I was – twenty years old and two years in, serving old people coffee without a single smile, pushed down by every manager in the building, with no idea what to do with my life. I toyed with the idea of training to be a speech therapist simply because I felt I'd be good at it, but even then, I had no idea how to apply to study for it. I was a waitress, on minimum wage, the rare gig with my second band my only escape. *What if I'd just told my parents I was going to study music production?* was a thought I had more than once during that time. *Would I have wanted to go to university then? Would I be producing my own music? Would I be working in a recording studio?*

And so herein lies my point – just as my dad has always said to me, despite my foolish decision many years ago to not listen – your life is *yours*, and yours alone. At the end of the day, I believe I was destined to take this path to where I am now – I *have* to believe that – but I spent years regretting my decision not to follow a career path I would've actually been happy in, instead doing what I believed would be 'best' for me. I spent many hours of my life thinking, *What if?* in actual tears, fearing I'd thrown my life away. Do not be me. Your life is still going to be yours long after (forgive me) your parents are gone, and then you'll be left with the career that they wanted for you. Sure, you might be earning enough, but will you be happy once you have no one left to please? When it comes to your future, give it your all, and answer only to yourself. Any alternative will lead to unhappiness, and success isn't measured in riches.

In your family's defence, and in my own family's, too, your parents only want you to succeed. Whether they want you to take academic subjects, or go into the family business, or try to force you into piano lessons which you think suck, they only want what they believe is best for you, because they care about you. It can be hard to see that when you're fighting them for what you love, and can lead to feelings of resentment, but you have a very special word in your vocabulary – *no*. Believe me, your parents won't like hearing it, especially if it's just that one word, but with the knowledge that you have the power to control what courses you take, what job you go into, what hobbies you have, you can reason with them as best you can.

Firstly, don't yell, 'NO! I WON'T DO IT!' and storm out. That's not going to get you anywhere. Sit down with your parents, as I wish I'd done, and treat them as human beings, instead of 'Mum and Dad'. Explain as best you can that this is what you want to do, how happy it will make you, and, whilst there's always the chance you might fall flat on your face, you have to give it a shot. A job, a course, a hobby, whatever it is – you have control over every single thing that requires your signature. In time, they will see how much heart you're putting into something you love, and perhaps they'll come round to the idea of you controlling your own destiny. If not, well . . . get them to read this section. Get them to read over my story of regret, and ask them how they would feel if they were in your position. Perhaps they secretly had dreams of their own which they sacrificed along the way.

Through hard work, I did get into the music business, despite having no qualifications. However, although I believe that the music production course would've helped me along the way (I still can't record music the way that course would've taught me) the path I did walk down – and the hard work that I put in – ended up leading me to the dream that I'd always had. Who knows? Perhaps if I had taken the music production course, I would never have taken up a job in waitressing and wouldn't have started making YouTube videos. Ultimately, my advice is this: always follow your heart. If you have a dream, and know of a way to start achieving it, then go for it. Always do your very best to chase after what you seek. Your decisions will affect the rest of your life. Live for you, because at the end of the day, when things are bleak – you are all you have.

The First Hurdle

Congratulations! You got rejected! Wait, what?

Who celebrates being rejected for something? you might ask. Well, I do – and so should you. Here are the reasons why:

> ⚡ If you don't celebrate, what else can you do? Be miserable and let it affect your confidence, that's what. When my first band was rejected at two separate Battle of the Bands competitions, it was really hard for me to bounce back. Being told you're not good once is hard enough, but twice in the space of a few months? That rejection can really get inside your head if you let it. *Maybe they know something I don't. Maybe I'm as bad as they say, and I'm just in denial.* Look, we all have that annoying voice in the back of our heads. You know the one – I have it, you have it, your friends and family have it, your worst enemy has it – the one that constantly makes you doubt yourself and is the cause of every occasion you've given up on something. Give it a name (a stupid one at that) so that it's not a part of you. The second you start listening to that voice and take it seriously, you're heading down a bad path. That little voice will get louder, and harsher, and bully you into not continuing with your passion. It will tell you that

you're not good enough, and that you're wasting your time, along with everyone else's. Shut it out from day one, and if you can already hear it, make a stand and refuse to listen any longer.

❧ Celebrate the fact that you've been rejected, rather than cry about it, because you had the guts to apply for something in the first place – meaning you had enough self-conviction to put yourself out there. Keep that level of confidence, and hold on to it – you'll need it in order to get back up again. There will be times in your life when you have to be your own cheerleader, because no one else will want to be. Dust yourself off, get back up, block out that voice and work even harder. You *will* see the fruits of your labours, even if it turns out to be in ways you never expected.

❧ It's practice. Everything you do is practice. The more often you do something, the better you get at doing it. Whether you've written a manuscript for a book that got rejected (you think what you're reading right now is the first draft? Really?) or applied for a talent show and been turned down, you put yourself out there, did something you loved and got feedback on it. You've been given advice on how to improve, even if the letter or email you received didn't

actually say what you did badly – you now
know that at that moment, what you gave
wasn't good enough. It sucks, I know, but take
what you created, tweak it, go over it again and
again, pick it apart and figure out what could've
been done better. In both Battle of the Bands
competitions, my voice was so shaky from nerves
at performing in front of strangers that I sounded
like an out-of-tune bleating sheep. Looking back,
I was *so* hard on myself! Of *course* I'd be nervous!
After that second rejection, I made a mental note
to myself that no future auditions would ever be
my first, and that next time I'd be equipped with
a foundation of experience – I'd know what to do
better in order to prevent the same outcome. And
if I failed again? Well, I'd come back even more
prepared.

❧ What's the worst that could happen? No rejection
can physically stop you from doing what you
love – you can still act if you didn't get that dream
role. You can still write novels if you didn't get
published straight away. The worst thing that
could happen after your being rejected is you
giving up, and, unlike rejection, that's solely on
you. Believe me, after being turned down for
many things (roles in the school play, the school

talent contest when I was eleven, a YouTube network when I first applied for a partnership) you kind of get used to the word 'no'. It always sucks, but after a while, you'll find yourself able to turn your dejection into passion and determination. You have two choices after being turned down – you can either take rejection to heart, or you can take critique on-board and refuse to give up. Either of these options will stop you feeling rejected, but only one will result in you regretfully wondering, *What if?*

It's all subjective! You may get turned down for something by one person or company, and then get accepted for the same thing by someone else! Let's take a classic, almost clichéd example – what do J.K. Rowling, U2 and the Beatles have in common? They were all famously rejected for their work. Could you imagine being the publisher that turned down *Harry Potter*? Could you fathom being the record label that said no to the freakin' BEATLES?! The fact is, the people they reached out to simply didn't believe their work would go anywhere – and they were very, very wrong. Keep applying for things, even if you fear getting rejected again – you may find you're the perfect fit.

Ask For Answers

(This section is named after a song by Placebo. For heaven's sake, go and listen to Placebo, and not just the singles. I'm not being paid to say that, they're just freakin' good.)

When it comes to asking others for help, I have three traits that go against me – I am introverted, I am stubborn, and I am proud. This can be a fatal combination when it comes to asking for someone's help, advice or feedback. I'm the sort of driver that will never stop and ask for directions (and thank goodness we live in a time of GPS) because I'm afraid of looking like a fool. I am constantly afraid of asking for advice in case the person I'm asking goes away thinking I am an idiot. However, when it comes to your work, and getting what you want, you *have* to call in favours. When I joined my first band, I would incessantly post about our upcoming gigs on my Facebook wall, inviting every single person on my friends list (yes, even the ones that lived abroad) to come to a show. When I released my first solo EP, I posted a link to it on all kinds of forums, hoping someone, *somewhere* would give it a listen. When I started my YouTube channel, I showed my first videos to everyone I knew – my co-workers, my bosses, my friends, my family – I wasn't embarrassed. I was proud. I turned the pride that usually prevented me from asking for help into pride in my own creations – I threw myself into promoting every single little thing that I made, telling anyone and everyone that this was the *best stuff yet* because I was happy with what I was sharing. I even remember asking my YouTube inspirations to check out my channel. They didn't, but I felt as though I'd given it my all, that I couldn't have done better, and wanted to share that feeling with the world.

Call it cliché, or call it realistic – this is a dog-eat-dog world. If you want something, you need to make connections. Do favours for others, and ask for nothing in return – the chances are that most people will remember if you've helped them in a time of need, and are likely to return the favour in kind later on down the line. If you want feedback on your work, then you have to seek it, and the best way to get it is through asking your peers. By September 2012, I had amassed 2,000 subscribers on my YouTube channel, and, whilst I was still trying to push my luck and spamming my favourite creators with my videos, I had also befriended a fellow creator called Gerard Groves. Gerard had 4,000 subscribers on his own channel, and whenever we'd upload, we'd give each other feedback and encouragement, as well as share each other's work. Five years on, Gerard and I are still close friends – I produce content for an audience on a bigger scale, and Gerard produces content for a very famous television broadcasting house. Without his constant encouragement, I don't know if I would've improved, or once again thrown in the towel on something I loved. Eventually towards the end of 2012, my channel did grab the attention of larger channels, but without getting that initial feedback from a peer, whose only goal was to encourage me to continue improving on my creations, and working hard to improve my editing and comedic timing, I don't know where I'd be today.

The lesson here is that if your work isn't noticed straight away, don't give up! Keep pushing, keep promoting the work you're proud of, always look to improve, swallow your pride and ask that friend with a good connection to help you out. Tweet out your portfolio or showreel – do whatever you need to do to make your dreams come true. Also, when that friend asks you for help, return the favour. Never forget the people who helped you start out – always aim to bring your peers up with you, just as you would want your peers to do for you if the roles were reversed.

The Little Picture

Ah, the *end goal*. Okay, firstly, let's just get it out there – there is no *end goal*. Your life isn't a Hollywood movie that lasts ninety minutes and ends with you kissing your love interest. Life will continue after you've achieved what you wanted – and then comes the next goal, and then the next. Whether your goal is a career, retiring with lots of money, or simply being whatever 'happy' is to you, there is always something else you can do to further it. This is why it is so important not to focus on one 'big picture' – it is the *middle* goals that you need to dedicate your life to accomplishing, not the *end goal*.

It is so, so important to be proud of every single achievement, whether it is big or small. Say you want to be an artist – whether that's living off commissions, having work displayed in a gallery, or being an illustrator for children's books. You should not wait to celebrate until you have achieved those specific end goals – that's an awfully long time to play down your small successes! Celebrate every little box that you tick from your to-do list – celebrate having saved up enough money to buy that sweet-ass set of paints or pens you saw online. Celebrate your first commission! Celebrate every single time you add something to your portfolio. I high-five myself every time I come up with a new chorus for a song, even if I can't figure out the rest. I rejoice every time I come up with a good joke in a video, let alone every time I finish editing and uploading! Every single new subscriber is a person I have entertained enough to have them click on a button that says 'I want more'. You have to see every little goal you complete as a step forward towards a bigger goal – you cannot feasibly hope to achieve what is in the 'big picture' without completing lots of little pictures first. Of course, the big picture is what drives you to keep moving forward – but don't forget to be kind to yourself every time you do something that gets you closer to the main goal that you want to achieve.

Oh, and also, if you have a setback, don't worry about it. If you need to take time out from your hard work to give your mental health a check-over, absolutely do it. Unfortunately, as we all know, employers don't see mental health as being as important as physical health – of course you can take unpaid leave for a broken leg, but depression? Forget about it. Just remember that even though, yes, your time on this planet is finite, your dreams can wait until you're back at your best. You will be happier with the work you have created when you are at full capacity. Be proud of yourself for taking necessary breaks which can help you reflect and see things from a new perspective, as that's also a positive step towards your goal. Forgive yourself for mistakes, celebrate rejection, and when you're feeling up to it again, jump back on the wagon and get back to those little pictures.

What If You Don't Know What You Want?

As I've already touched upon, at school and college I always felt as though I was the only person who had no idea of what they wanted to do for the rest of their life. Let's go back to calling the idea of being a performer a 'pipe dream', which is often how it felt to me growing up. There was nothing else in the world that held my interest, yet being a singer seemed out of reach. Whilst my friends were taking courses in business studies to become accountants, art to be architects, law to be ... well, you get it; no matter how hard I tried, I couldn't convince myself that I wanted to do anything full-time except for singing. I certainly went through phases where I considered career paths that I *might* enjoy – there was a two-week period of my life that I wanted to become a paramedic, simply because I'd read a book written by one. My sudden 'passion' for a potential career path would fizzle out, only to be replaced with an idea just as fleeting. Over the joint seven years I spent in secondary school and college, I was given countless 'career meetings' – which in my experience were all useless wastes of time where you sit opposite someone you've never met, who pretends to know everything about you from the piece of paper in front of them with your grade predictions on it and then proceeds to say something along the lines of, 'It says here you're predicted an A in English language – have you considered becoming an English teacher?'

(Perhaps your experience of 'career meetings' will be better than mine, but whatever subject I was succeeding in, the advisors all suggested that I should become a teacher in that subject. I'm starting to wonder if all of my meetings were secretly funded by a teachers' board or something.)

If you are like I was, with no seemingly achievable goals, I urge you to do what I *didn't do* for a long time, and just follow your passion. Don't be modest – there's something in the world that makes you happy. Start thinking about careers to do with the thing you love the most: say you're good at English, but don't massively enjoy it, and love video games but aren't that great at playing them. Combine the two and work towards being a video-game journalist. If you enjoy horse riding, and nothing much else, screw it! Your heart is in horse riding – do something to do with horse riding. Train to be a jockey, or make it your goal to own stables. Your goals do not have to be career-based – that's very important to remember. Of course, sceptics reading this will say things such as, 'Emma, you can't tell everyone to follow their dreams, because not *everyone* can achieve them.' But let me tell you this – no one who has ever truly followed their heart has regretted it, even if it's ended in a less than desirable outcome. I'm not going to sit here with the opportunity to tell you to chase your dreams and then go against it – if you love something, follow it with all of your heart.

Also, make sure to bear in mind that you may not have this whole 'life' thing figured out at the same time as other people, but that doesn't mean you'll never find a career path that you enjoy. People discover their talents and passions at different times throughout their lives – it's just that the pressures of completing education at a young age make us believe that it all has to be figured out by the age of sixteen. I only developed a love for professional wrestling when I turned nineteen, after stumbling upon a YouTube video that used clips of a CM Punk vs John Cena match over the top of a soundtrack to a show I enjoyed watching. From then on, I was hooked, going to every London show I could, watching it weekly as though it were my religion, and even dreaming of being a wrestler myself! (This dream faded away when I realised that wrestling is for the extremely fit individual with an extremely high pain tolerance – but perhaps one day, if I decide to take my life down a different path, I'll work towards a job writing storylines or controlling the social media platforms for my favourite wrestling company. Who knows? If I want to do something that badly, I'll chase it, at any cost. I hope you will do the same.)

It's actually quite funny to me thinking back to 2005, when I was thirteen, surrounded by kids in my class who knew exactly what they wanted to do with their lives. YouTube was only founded in 2005, and being a full-time vlogger wouldn't become a thing for many years. I never could have predicted that this would be somewhat of my 'calling' in 2012. It can take years for you to discover a job you'd love to do, so if you're young, and feeling under pressure to pick subjects to study, go with what you *enjoy* – the right path will eventually unfold, even if it takes longer for you than it does for your friends.

Whatever you do, don't panic. Remember that success isn't defined by how much you earn, or how high you can climb up a corporate ladder – it is determined by your happiness every night when your head hits your pillow. Aim to be so in love with your job that it doesn't feel like work – and if you don't know how to get there just yet, you will in time. Follow your dreams, and if you don't know what they are, keep searching for them. They'll come around, and probably in ways you never imagined. If you find yourself doing a job that doesn't make you happy – do not be quick to write yourself off. I know from first-hand experience that when you start to tell yourself that you are stuck in a job with no way out, you will no longer believe you are worthy of better things. Keep working hard towards your goals by any means necessary – in any instance you have some time to yourself, work on making contacts in your dream vocation and getting experience with them, helping them out and learning along the way. It can be exhausting taking on extra work when you're committed to a full-time job to make ends meet – but you get one life. You owe it to yourself to make it the best life that you can.

Also, whilst I had many negative experiences in my previous jobs, there were definitely some benefits from doing all of them. I made some wonderful friends and have some great memories – and I also learned an awful lot about the real world. You may not be able to begin following your dreams right away, and there will be times in your life when you may simply have to buckle down and do a less-than-desirable job in order to pay the bills, but in the meantime, you will learn how to survive, keep your head down when rumours and gossip spread, how to smile and be polite in the face of the rudest people – and knowing you have it in you to survive a shitty experience is something you can be proud of.

2

The Brain Stuff

Warning: This chapter covers a lot of sensitive topics concerning mental health, and is a heavy read. If you wish to proceed, only read when you feel calm and comfortable. If you wish to skip this section, the next chapter is on page 72.

You made it past Chapter One! Oh, I'm so relieved that you've enjoyed what I've written so far. Let me be absolutely clear, before anybody gets the wrong idea – whilst I am definitely a much stronger, happier person than I was many years ago, my journey continues. I am not *always* happy, and my mind is not always as clear as it is on the day that I am writing the introduction to this chapter. I have my good days with my mental health, but I also have my bad days – as does everyone. The following segments in this chapter go into greater detail about my struggles with my mental health, such as depression and anxiety. They were not easy to write, and so they may not be easy to read. Nevertheless, I wanted to include this small introduction to stress a point: in no way, shape or form does having any kind of a mental health issue make you less worthy of love and care than anyone without one. Some days will be very hard to get through, but even the world's leading health professionals are making new discoveries about the brain all of the time. You are not a failure if you have a mental health issue. Along the way, you will encounter people who will try to write you (and your problems) off, as though only physically visible afflictions are valid. Over the years I have been told many a time to 'man up', 'get over it', 'smile more' and, of course, 'just stop thinking about it'. I used to get angry at the people behind those words, but after hearing them so many times, I now turn my frustration into the love I wish I was shown during my hardest times – I turn the other cheek, laugh inwardly at their ignorance and walk away, hoping and praying they never have to struggle with a mental health issue of their own. Of course, not everyone reading this book will struggle with mental health issues, and I am truly so happy for those individuals. However – my struggles have shaped me into a wiser, stronger person. With every pit I fall down, my arms get stronger as I claw my way back out again. I am who I am today because of what I have been through. I wrote the following segments a few months before I wrote this introduction, and I have chosen to leave them frozen in that moment of time, unedited and raw for you to read. I believe they will give you a better insight into my mind and explain how I have come to be the strong, independent woman that I am today.

Anxiety: My Story

Fuck, I don't want to start this chapter. I've been putting it off for hours. I've been trying to distract myself by watching YouTube videos and passively snacking. I've had the video of Shia LaBeouf telling me to 'just do it!' on repeat for well over an hour. Fuck, I don't want to write about this, I don't want to think about this, I don't want to give this *thing* the satisfaction of acknowledging its presence and impact on my life – but I have to. I promised myself I would write about this, and finally go into detail about the mental health problem that I've struggled with for almost ten years.

I suffer with a very specialised form of anxiety.

I say 'suffer' – that's not strictly true anymore. I certainly used to 'suffer', but I'm finally at a point in my life where I can (almost) peacefully co-exist with it. I can manage it. However, this anxiety has defined almost half of my entire life – my later teenage years and early adulthood were all led by this horrid, self-destructive beast that lived rent-free in my brain.

I don't want to write about it, I don't want to make my brain think it is okay for it to repeat what I've been through, but I've been learning to fight against my instincts since I was seventeen years old. So fuck my fear – I'm going to write about it.

When I was ten years old, I was on holiday with my parents in Gran Canaria, one of the Canary Islands not far from the coast of Morocco. It was the second (and final) holiday I had with both of my parents, and I was having the time of my life – going to all the little clubs for kids at the resort, swimming in the big pool outside our room, visiting the water parks – until my dad collapsed.

My dad collapsing was a culmination of his ears popping on the departing flight due to cabin pressure, and the sheer boiling Macaronesian heat. He was sitting outside our hotel room on a deckchair in the shade when he began to feel unwell. As soon as he stood up, he collapsed, hitting his head on the hard patio. My mum shooed me away to one of the resort clubs as she shouted for help, and I ran off, confused, thinking my dad was just playing around. After all – my dad had been perfectly fine and healthy for all of my life. Nothing ever went wrong with my dad. I skipped off down towards the kids' club early, knowing that so long as I did what my mum told me to do, everything would be okay.

My dad was treated by doctors, and felt better almost immediately, but the rest of the trip was tainted. After we flew back home, my dad's health declined. He began to feel dizzy and would collapse without notice. For the next two years between the ages of ten and twelve, I had to endure the long, nervous trips back and forth to the hospital, waiting outside private rooms with my mum whilst they conducted test after test, first incorrectly diagnosing him with epilepsy, then meningitis, then telling us that he had a heart condition – none of which turned out to be the right diagnosis.

After two years of being misdiagnosed and incorrectly given all sorts of pills that made him ten times worse, he was finally diagnosed with vertigo, caused by a fault in the balance mechanism of the inner ear. He began to take medication to get it under control, and things returned to (almost) normal. However – during these two long, agonising years watching my mother cry almost every day, I began to realise that my parents were not as immortal as I'd once believed. Up until this point, my dad had been a superhero with zero weaknesses, impervious to illness and someone who would be around for ever. Now, to twelve-year-old Emma, he was simply mortal. He was someone who could get ill, and *would* get ill – eventually to the point where he wouldn't be able to fight any more.

My dad's illness took its toll on my parents' marriage, and shortly after I turned twelve, my mum and dad separated. Due to my parents' work and childcare arrangements, I was always a little bit closer to my dad than I was to my mum, and so I stayed with my dad. Now it was just Dad and me. Over the course of the next few years, through secondary school, in part due to the fact that I was a complete loner, we began to rely solely on each other for support. My dad was (and always has been) my best friend. As his condition improved and was managed by medication, my fears about his mortality slowly retreated to the back of my mind, until I no longer thought about it.

Until the day that I did.

I was seventeen years old when I had my first blow of anxiety. I was lying in bed, trying to get to sleep. Usually, I'd have no problem falling asleep (I'm the type to pass out the second my head hits the pillow) but for some reason on that fateful night, my mind was fully awake. I still remember the exact thought that flashed through my brain, seemingly from out of nowhere, and the horrid feeling of being metaphorically struck by a freight train as I processed it.

'Your dad is going to die.'

You know the expression 'his blood ran cold'? The metaphor that you read in crime thrillers which tells you something bad is about to happen? I found out that night that it isn't just a metaphor. Almost immediately after my mind conjured up that simple phrase, presented as a fact, I felt the blood in my veins turn to ice. I no longer felt warm. My heart began to pound in my chest as I lay there, unable to move, my skin breaking out in a sweat as though it were burning hot, when I was actually ice cold. I felt as though I needed to be sick. I felt my stomach twist, as though it was being wrung out like a dishcloth by two tightly squeezing hands, before feeling it plummet to where my intestines were. I felt my cheeks burning hot whilst the rest of my body shivered, prickling as though being jabbed by tiny little needles. I suddenly felt light-headed and as though I was no longer on the planet I once felt safe on. The simple phrase 'Your dad is going to die' burned its way on to my retinas, repeating itself over and over like the incessant demands of a child as I lay there hyperventilating, trying to stay quiet so as not to wake up my dad sleeping in the next room. My dad was going to die. I was going to live to see my dad die. My dad wasn't going to be around for all my life. My dad was going to have a heart attack. He was going to be alone, trying to call for an ambulance, when he would no longer be able to breathe, and *he was going to die.* Mental images flashed through my brain a million miles a minute, making me envision my dad, my best friend, lying on the floor, *dead.* I began to cry, still shaking, still feeling as though I was going to be sick, until eventually I was able to steady my breathing and fall asleep, my brain finally exhausted.

This was the first time in my life that I had experienced a panic attack. It didn't happen again the next night, or the next – but unluckily for me, this attack wasn't an isolated incident.

Before these attacks started happening (which was only ever at night when my brain was idle and I was alone), I would listen to music with noise-cancelling headphones on, letting myself be carried away by my favourite songs so that I could be happy and at peace before going to sleep. After that first attack, I couldn't do it anymore. *What if, when you're listening to a song, your dad starts having a heart attack, and cries out for you to call an ambulance, but you don't hear him because of your headphones? What if his last moment on earth is him crying out for help, and his daughter ignoring him?*

Over time, these attacks decided that they would no longer be confined to the brief moments before sleep. My dad is almost always by his phone and, nine times out of ten, picks up after about three rings. Every time I called him, whether it was from college, work, or whenever I wasn't near him, I would count the rings. My anxiety would heighten with every additional ring that went unanswered. After five rings, I knew he wasn't going to pick up, and immediately, in my mind, he was *dead*. He was lying on the floor, motionless, *dead*. As soon as I heard the automated voicemail instead of my dad's voice, an attack would occur. Immediately, my heart rate would soar and my stomach would plummet, I would sweat, my blood would run cold, my cheeks would prickle – and I had to get out of whatever room I was in. Whatever the size of the room, it was too small. This would happen at YouTube parties, on dates at restaurants with my then-boyfriend – wherever I was, on the rare occasion my dad wouldn't pick up the phone, I would spiral into an attack without fail. I would ring his spare phone, and if he didn't answer, I would phone my mum, who at this point lived nearby and could pop over to his house to check on him. After a few minutes of enduring an attack, my phone would vibrate, and I would look down and see my dad's number.

'Sorry, pup,' he would answer. 'I left my phone in the bathroom. How's your evening going?'

This form of separation anxiety continued for years. Just before my anxiety began, I had finally decided that if music wasn't going to work out for me, I would study for a PhD in linguistics, and eventually become a researcher for speech development in children. It was something we had studied briefly in college, and I had finally begun to feel as though I could do something other than music for the rest of my life – but now, thanks to the cycle my brain would go into every time it was idle, I wasn't even going to apply to go. I took a 'gap year' and worked in restaurants for the next three years instead. I said no to holidays and nights out with the few friends I had finally made, out of fear that, as soon as I was away, my dad would fall ill and *die* without me there. The fear of my dad falling ill and dying very quickly took over my entire life, and every life decision was based around it. Boyfriends would witness me having an attack and think I was 'crazy'. Friends would frown and say, 'You can't think like that!' as though my mind gave me any form of choice. No matter how many times I tried to tell myself not to panic, I was fighting a losing battle against my brain, putting my adult life on hold as I became a slave to my own thoughts.

When I was twenty-one and my YouTube was beginning to take off, I was having a meeting with my management team in London when the topic of me visiting America came up. I immediately shut down the idea. 'No, no,' I said. 'I can't. I can't leave the UK.' I was asked to explain my issues, and so I did. My YouTube manager was extremely sympathetic, but told me in no uncertain terms that I was going to waste a whole lot of opportunities if I didn't seek help. She spoke to the father of one of her colleagues, who was a doctor, and managed to pull some strings in order to get me a free session. Explaining my entire backstory to a total stranger is still up there as one of the most terrifying things I have ever done – as soon as I began talking, I burst into tears.

'I think it's quite clear that your brain has got itself caught in a loop, causing it to act extremely irrationally,' he said. 'I'm going to prescribe you some medication, and we'll see if that helps to unravel the knot.' I'm not about to sit here and judge this doctor for prescribing me medication only an hour after meeting me – every doctor works differently. Should he instead have focused on getting to the root of the problem, rather than sticking me on meds and hoping for the best? Possibly – but the medication did have an effect. Over time, I began to find that I could go a few more phone rings before my panic would set in, and before too long I was able to fight my go-to irrationality with rational thoughts. *He is not dead*, I would tell myself as my heart tried to race. *He has done this before. He has left his phone in the bathroom, or it's on silent and he can't hear it. He's mowing the lawn and can't hear it. He is fine. Give it a few moments.*

Whilst this didn't always work, and the attacks would some-times break their way through, the medication – along with the support from my then-boyfriend – began to allow me to live a semi-normal life. I began to agree to go on trips away from my home town for more than one night, and I started to attend YouTube events in America. Slowly but surely, my anxiety became manageable, and eventually I was able to come off the medication and still go through the steps that calmed me down. In the summer of 2016, I finally bit the bullet and did the thing that I wanted to do when I was eighteen – I moved out of my home town, eighty miles away from my family. At first, it was hell on my anxiety – now, if there was a family emergency, I was hours away, just as I'd feared I'd be if I went to university – but over time, I began to realise that the increased distance between me and my dad wouldn't affect the likelihood of something happening. The breakthrough point for me was being able to view my anxiety attacks as irrational – once I was able to recognise that my brain was acting irrationally, and would soon return to normal, I was able to begin to defeat that bad train of thought that had led to the panic attack.

I still have my bad moments. If my dad hasn't answered the phone after about ten minutes, and my mum can't get through to him either, I'll start to panic. The telltale signs of restlessness and an increased heart rate kick in, despite my telling myself that there is a perfectly reasonable explanation for him not picking up the phone. There might come a day when my dad will not answer the phone and something *will* be terribly wrong, or I'll receive a call from my mum (my mum and I prefer to text, so whenever I see her number come up on my screen, I immediately jump to the conclusion that something bad has happened), but for the most part, I'm ready. Thanks to this irrational separation anxiety, I have essentially mourned my dad's death for eight years. I have seen images of him on the floor of his living room, alone, dead from a heart attack. I have seen images of me boxing up his belongings. For eight years, I have had to listen to my mind say, *He's dead, he's dead, he's dead and alone and you're not there*, and I truly believe that one of the reasons I have been able to (for the most part) conquer my anxiety is because I mentally tortured myself to the point where I simply couldn't exist with it any longer. Of course, I am fortunate that I was able to overcome the brunt of my anxiety with medication and persistence, but there is absolutely zero shame in seeking therapy. Trained professionals will have seen many cases such as yours over the years, because you are not alone in your struggle – but each case is unique to the individual. Trial and error, met with a lot of persistence and determination to find a way to manage your mental health issue, will eventually result in you discovering the treatment that is right for you.

The fact is – and this is what I tell myself when I feel an attack bubbling in my chest – worrying simply does nothing. Sometimes, my instinct to worry is out of my control and unavoidable, but worrying in itself only produces negative effects, with no benefits. When my heart is racing, I ask myself, 'Will panicking about this problem make the solution come quicker?' and the answer is always no. This can be frustrating when you are worrying so much that you cannot calm down by your own command, but I've found that asking myself this question often injects a dose of rationality into my irrationally-acting brain.

This ability to isolate my panic and fear and identify them as separate entities that cause harm has also had long-term benefits. One day, my parents will be dead. There will come a time in my life where I will exist without them. Whilst that knowledge used to paralyse me, and rock me to my core, it is now a fact that I have come to terms with and accept. It *will* happen, and I've seen it over and over again in my mind – and whilst I'll never be truly ready for it, I know that I'm as hardened as I can be for doomsday. Birthdays are still difficult – every year on my dad's birthday, the only thought I have racing through my mind all day is, *Is this the age he will be when he dies*? The (almost) funny part is that over the course of eight years, these have been my thoughts:

'Will sixty-three be the age my dad dies?'

'Will sixty-four be the age my dad dies?'

'Will sixty-five be the age my dad dies?'

'Will sixty-six be the age my dad dies?'

And so on, and so forth. My point is, worrying does nothing. Despite my worrying, my dad has continued to live, in good shape and in reasonable health. One day he won't be around anymore. It is going to happen, it will be unavoidable, and it will be awful – but worrying about it won't stop it from happening. Refusing to go to university didn't make him immortal. Staying at home when my friends were on holiday didn't change the fact that one day, he will be gone. In this sense, in being able to battle my fear and no longer letting it control me, I have beaten my monster. I don't believe my monster will ever disappear entirely – for me, my anxiety is a dragon, that is for now perfectly sound asleep at the back of my mind, but which could wake up at any moment. However, if you'd told me eight years ago that I would be travelling the world, living away from my home town and no longer collapsing to the floor when my dad didn't pick up the phone, the terrified, half-alive human that I once was would never have believed you.

To be honest with you, I'm not entirely sure how to relate this back to any of you guys out there who also struggle with anxiety, because as I said before: all cases are unique to the individual. All I can say is that regardless of the form of anxiety, I understand how hard that uphill battle towards a clearer mind is. I have lost entire weeks of sleep. I have had mental images of my parents that no child should have to see. I have been at war with a voice in my head that is still trying to work against me to this day. I have endured the pain of trying to explain this irrationality to friends, strangers, professionals and, hardest of all, my dad. How do you tell your dad that your brain is restricting your ability to live because it imagines him dead?

I haven't walked a mile in your shoes, but I can appreciate how tired your feet are. Stay stubborn. Fight your own brain, and refuse to give in. Talk to a professional at the first given opportunity. Don't be afraid to try medication. (My own meds, despite helping long-term, had awful side effects that made me extremely irritable and depressed – those side effects are not your fault. If you can't handle them, go back to your doctor and tell them, and demand they prescribe you an alternative.) Write out your irrational thoughts and look at them when you're feeling calm, so that you can begin to see they're not rational. Most importantly – you are not beyond help. You are not hopelessly 'crazy', no matter how many people will try to make you feel that way. Hang around with people that will support you instead of mocking you. I thought I would feel this way for ever – and perhaps my dragon will awaken again one day – but even the hardest of times are temporary. You are not alone. Anxiety and panic disorders are more common than ever in our increasingly stressful society. Do not be afraid to seek help – there will be trained professionals (including those answering the helplines at the back of this book) who will understand that you have a mental health issue which is not your fault.

My life is now split into two halves – the half where my dad is alive, and the other half where he is no longer here. I am thankful that I am still in the first half, but I have spent a lot of it living in fear. Now, after years of struggling, enduring, panicking, crying, fighting, giving up, fighting all over again and finally taking control, I am living out the rest of that half enjoying however much time I have left with him. And, Dad, if you're reading this, there was nothing you could have done to prevent this happening. It was never anything you did. Just as we can fall and break our ankles, sometimes our brains can fail us, too. I love you. Just . . . stop leaving your phone somewhere out of your hearing range!

Dear anxiety

Three thousand seven hundred words ago, I was scared of writing about you. I was scared you'd come back if I acknowledged you as part of my history. I just fucking *wrote about you*, despite putting off this task for months, and I didn't cry. Not once. My heart didn't begin to race. I didn't have to step back and take a break. I wrote about you, fearlessly, because I'm not afraid of you anymore. I'm not anxious about feeling anxious. You don't control

me or my actions anymore. *I'm* the one in control now.
Your power over me is gone. Fuck you, and fuck what
you put me through. If you were a human, I would
wound you as much as you wounded me. I would make
you pay for what you did to me for so long, and how
you inhibited my thoughts, my lifestyle and my choices
over my future. Alas, I can't. I refuse to be 'thankful' for
you, for 'making me who I am today', or 'shaping me
into a strong human'. You stole eight years of my life.
You made me a prisoner of my own mind, and made
me envision possible scenarios which I can never un-see.
I would have grown to be strong without your 'help'.
I will never forgive you, but also – I will never let you
back in. I am battle-ready now. You were the monster
under my bed, but now, I'm in an entirely different
room altogether – away from you, away from my panic
attacks and irrational thoughts. You are done. Fuck you,
and goodnight. For good. I'm making sure of it.

I'm not scared of you any more.

Depression

Whilst I describe my anxiety as a fearsome dragon that might let
out a mighty roar at any given moment, that isn't how I would
describe my experience with depression. I do not envision my bouts
of depression as *angry* or *terrifying*; to me, my depression is more like
an injured bear, weeping and begging for my attention. I do not want
it there, and yet, when it cries, I cry too; when it wants my attention,
it has it, wholly and utterly. I put everything else aside for my injured

bear, wishing someone would put it out of its misery, or at the very least, take it away from me so I can no longer see it. I do not have the same hatred for my recurring depressive state as I do for my anxiety, which is oddly amusing to me, as I've struggled with depression for far longer. I think it has more to do with the fact that when I was at my lowest with anxiety, my dragon was always present; it *was* me, it consumed me entirely, but my injured bear only comes to visit every so often and I often know when to expect it, and therefore it has no element of surprise. A dragon comes roaring, baring its teeth and consuming my world in a blaze from its nostrils; an injured bear limps into view, slowly, with no energy to fight.

No two cases of depression are the same. My experience with depression will not be the same as yours, should you suffer with it. Your experience will be completely unique to you, but mine can be defined by a few traits which consume my mind for up to months at a time:

> ❧ Lethargy. I sleep more. I sleep all day. When I am awake, I am tired. I am tired when I work, I am tired when I do nothing.
>
> ❧ Apathy. I have no desire to better myself, nor do I care to look after myself. I will binge-eat junk food, and to hell with the consequences. I will shut myself off from the world, and very quickly go from 'treating myself' to days in bed watching YouTube videos and eating snacks to purposely

cutting off friends and cancelling my planned
hangouts with them. In full bloom, talking with
my friends in little doses brings me joy, but when
I am depressed, I want nothing more than to be
alone. The thought of confiding in my friends
both scares and disgusts me. I will often go for
weeks without making the effort to see anyone,
preferring to be alone than to share my misery.

- Self-loathing. I begin to compare myself to others
  in an entirely different way. Whilst the colours
  of my world begin to desaturate into black and
  white, I see my peers in brighter colours than
  ever before, taking in every perfect aspect of their
  personalities and wishing I could be as happy
  and successful as them. I begin to scrutinise
  everything I do, and impostor syndrome takes
  hold; in my mind, I am a fraud, I am talentless
  and have zero worth. Everything I do is, to
  me, a catastrophic failure. I consider myself
  unsuccessful and irrelevant in my fields of work,
  both with YouTube and music. This is often
  accompanied by a lot of crying.

- Lack of creativity. My job relies heavily on me
  being able to come up with original ideas and
  putting passion behind everything I do. When I
  am depressed, I lose the will to care about what I

make, and cannot for the life of me come up with any original ideas. If you look at my YouTube channel over the course of the last five years, you can actually see a pattern: I will upload a certain genre of video for months on end, and then not upload for a while. After about a month or so, I will return, rejuvenated, with new ideas and full of passion once again. That month of silence was spent sitting in bed, comparing myself to others, calling myself a failure and crying.

However, with every cycle of extreme happiness followed by a wave of depression, I become better equipped for my injured bear. Having struggled with bouts of depression since the age of thirteen, I have become able to detect when a depressive wave is coming. It's sort of like how animals can detect an impending earthquake and flee the vicinity of impact, only I can't run away. I know it is approaching, and there is little to nothing I can do about it. The night before a depressive state takes hold, I just feel *off*. It's hard to describe it to anyone, but when you've lived in your own body for so long, you know when something isn't right. Sometimes, my depressive state is triggered by an event, and other times, my injured bear will just turn up and expect me to sit and whimper with it until it feels satisfied with its received sympathy and waddles away for a little while, only to return when it feels lonely and neglected for too long.

When I first battled depression, I didn't know what it was. I'd heard the term before, but even just twelve years ago, when I was thirteen, it wasn't as widely accepted as a mental health issue as it is today (and of course, we still have a long way to go in terms of educating young people and teaching them that mental health issues are common and not to be stigmatised). I was hurting from my parents' separation, more so than I'd let on to either of them; I was succeeding at school, but was teased and bullied by my peers for being 'ugly', 'greasy' and a 'dirty emo'; my crush didn't like me back, the kids I thought were cool didn't want to know me – I was completely and utterly alone. Whilst school was my escape from my situation at home, home was my escape from my school situation. I was unhappy in both of the places I was forced to be, on top of trying to deal with adolescence and all of the hormones and insecurities that come with it – and so I acted out.

I began going to the local skate park at weekends, listening to heavy metal and drinking cheap wine, becoming romantically involved with anyone who showed me the slightest bit of affection and doing anything I could to feel happy, even just for a split second. I don't even really remember when that first depressive state lifted. When I was fifteen, my half-sister Febe was born, and I remember that being a huge turning point in the broken-down relationship I had with my mum. For a few years after she was born, and following the birth of my half-brother Travis, my mental state began to improve; I focused hard on doing well in my exams, trying hard to make my dad proud after rebelling against him for so many years. I went to college and finally found friends who made me feel appreciated for who I truly was, and I stopped trying to be somebody else; I bit the bullet and joined two different bands and finally began to take steps towards building a music career . . . and then I got stuck in a dead-end job.

Suddenly, that feeling of hopelessness came rushing back, as the new-job honeymoon phase died out and became stale-job melancholy. Feeling trapped and being forced to do things against my will is a surefire way of setting off my depression, and this time, my depression spiralled into anger. I lashed out at my boss, my co-workers, my customers, my parents, my friends – anything that would have slightly irked me before now enraged me. At twenty years old, for the first time since I was fifteen, I took up smoking again, after my supervisor offered me a cigarette. I would come home from work, sit in front of the TV, eat the dinner my dad had cooked me, and then go up to my room and cry, before going to bed just to wake up and do it all over again.

Although I love my current job more than I have ever loved working for someone else, my depression didn't simply go away after I became my own boss; in fact, due to the sudden reliance on my own creativity in order to make a living, the pressure I felt to be good at my 'job' soared through the roof. Suddenly, my job wasn't nine to five, but 24/7. I had to watch what I was saying, as well as post about my life enough to keep people engaged and interested but not too much so as not to annoy my audience, and come up with ideas that others had yet to think of, lest I be a 'copycat' of another creator. Any and every negative comment written about me, whether it was on one of my own videos or a forum where people would discuss me in the third person, would make my stomach drop. I had gone from making videos I enjoyed as a hobby for a few hundred people to having hundreds of thousands of people watch me and scrutinise every little thing I did or said. I was being called 'ugly' and 'annoying' by people who had never met me. Whilst I wish to stress how much happier I am doing what I do now, having what feels like the entire world criticising you and remembering your slip-ups does things to a fragile person. No job is without its downsides, and I do not ask for pity; this is the life I have chosen to lead.

With that said, since I became an 'online personality' (or 'YouTube sensation', as is the common tagline used by the media, which always makes me laugh. What does that even mean?), my depression has been in a constant state of come and go, as though my injured bear is stuck in a revolving door. I can be creative and happy for months, until one comment will send me spiralling, making me doubt everything I've ever made. Willingly putting my life out on the Internet for the world to see and scrutinise has seen my depression hit me in waves, as often as every couple of months and lasting for weeks or months at a time. However, just as with my anxiety, I have long since felt as 'in control' of my depression as I possibly can be. I can predict when it's about to happen, and I am aware that it is a temporary state of being; I know when to take it easy, and try to stick to goals and targets in order to feel accomplished and battle through my lethargy and apathy. If I can't create, I will force myself to do the admin work I've been putting off, such as emails and meetings. I will try my hardest not to back out of seeing friends, because I know I'll enjoy my time with them once we're actually hanging out, and company helps me put my life back into the right perspective. Most of all, I'm able to tell myself that this isn't my fault. I am *not* worthless, nor am I an untalented fraud – that is my injured bear trying to control me, and not who I am at the core of my being.

It has taken a lot of anguish to make peace with my depression and to allow it to wash over me before letting it leave again. I am not angry at my injured bear for always pestering me, because acting violently towards a bear will just make it act violently in return. Instead, I try and look on the bright side. I am thankful for my friends and family. I am so grateful for the freedom I have in being my own boss. I am not in poverty, nor am I in chronic pain. When I am depressed, it can be hard to see the positive things in my life, as they are so greatly overshadowed by the negativity that I let consume me, but the weeks and months of feeling lost and unhappy are nothing compared to that day when the dark fog finally lifts, and the world is no longer a dreary black and white.

I made a Feel Good 101 video on the topic of depression back in 2013. I still stand by what I said in that video, four years ago:

> Imagine you are walking in a forest. You are alone, there is no one around, and then suddenly, BAM! You trip and fall down a well that wasn't clearly marked, and you fall sixty feet down this well. You break your leg, and now there is a heavy rock on top of it. You can't move, and you are in pain, and all you can see is a little bit of light sixty feet above you, which you can't reach. There's no ladder to climb back up, so you are stuck down this well alone. That is what depression is. From here, you have two options. You can wait in pain for your broken leg to heal by itself, chip away at the rock, and then climb up the well with your hands and exhaust yourself – or you can shout so loud and for so long that someone who eventually walks past the well hears you and throws you a rope for you to use to climb back out.

I will say that 2013 Emma didn't state the obvious – that climbing up a rope with a broken leg would definitely still hurt – but option two is certainly more efficient than option one. Trying to fight through depression alone, especially when you do not know how to cope with the intensely negative feelings that come with it, can be extensive and often futile. Talk to someone. Demand help. There are trained professionals (including those on the helplines at the back of this book) who can and will help you. I will always recommend talking to your family if you feel as though you can, although I know just how tough that can be. Depression is still stigmatised, and still something we are taught to see as shameful, as though we are defective and a stain on the clean shirt of society. Listen to me: you are not a let-down. I can guarantee that there will be people you will confide in who will tell you to *get over it*, or tell you that you're *being silly*. If you are experiencing prolonged feelings of hopelessness, or contemplating self-harm or suicide, you are not being silly, and fuck anyone who thinks so. If your parents or doctors won't take you seriously, it can be soul-crushing – but keep going. Find someone who *will* take you seriously – including medical professionals if you can. I am fortunate to live in a country with free healthcare, but regardless of your situation, please make it your main priority to try and speak to a doctor or counsellor, and demand that they help you treat your depression. It's often talked about how we as a society see a broken leg as a medical emergency, but we do not perceive mental health issues to be just as severe, mostly due to their lack of physical symptoms upon first inspection. Throughout my teenage years, I never told my parents I felt depressed, even after I realised that's what I was going through, because I was terrified of their reactions. I was worried they would feel as though I'd let them down, or worse, that they'd let *me* down. I did my best to hide how miserable I was, and it wasn't their fault that I didn't feel as though I could confide in them – it was the shame that society made me feel for having a mental health problem. We are fortunate that we are developing into a society where the upcoming generation of parents is more aware of how common depression is, and that in our lifetime we will all hopefully be treating depression, anxiety and other mental health problems such as OCD and trichotillomania as legitimate illnesses, just as we do cancer and other physical conditions. It may take many years, but I am hopeful – we are learning more about the human brain every day due to progress in science and research, and hope will always lie with the youth; our ability to be open with our struggles and communicate openly about them is the only way to break the stigma of mental illness.

Listen to me: you are not alone. Whilst your depression is unique to you, and no one can live inside your head and truly understand what it is like being you, millions of people are living with the same condition as you at any given moment. You are not *weird*, you are not *being silly* or *being dramatic* – if you believe you have cause for concern, then run with it. Fight for your happiness, unashamedly and without fear. If you are young, living at home with your family, and too frightened to tell them that you are worried for your mental state, you can tear out the next page as a last resort and leave it with your parent or guardian:

Hello there

Your kid needs to talk with you. They are feeling
scared and overwhelmed, and are possibly suffering
from depression. This note wouldn't be left with
you unless they believed there was serious cause for
concern. Your child is not being dramatic or stupid –
depression is becoming increasingly common in
teenagers and young adults, and can start without
warning. Your child has left you this note because
they want to talk to you about how they're feeling,
and seek help in order to no longer feel as low as they
do. They trust you, and need your understanding,
kindness and support. Please do not dismiss their
feelings as 'being young', or lash out at them. Being
angry at them for confiding in you won't make their
situation any better. Your kid needs you right now.
Please go and talk to them and give them the support
they need.

As far as my own fight with depression goes – will I continue to have depressive cycles for the rest of my life? Will they go away if I choose to fade away from the Internet? Who knows? In the meantime – yes, my depression inhibits my life. It affects my relationships and creative drive, but you know what? As cheesy and as clichéd as it sounds, I am not defined by my depression. I am fortunate enough to be able to tell myself how temporary these feelings are whilst going through the worst of it – others may not be so lucky. If you think you may be suffering from depression, please seek help from a professional, and don't keep it bottled up out of fear of not being taken seriously. Fight as hard as you can until you find someone who will listen and be willing to help you. The battle will be more in your favour when you have an army behind you. Seek help, stay strong, fight back, and remember: you are not your illness.

Self-Harm

When I first laid out my plans for the topics to be covered in this book, I knew this one would be one of the most challenging. However, it is because it is still so difficult to talk about self-harm openly that it is important that I – and we as a society – *do* talk about it. For as long as I have been alive, and for many decades before that, the topic of self-harm has been considered taboo. The idea of someone taking out their frustrations and despair on their own body is still perceived as a relatively new concept, when in reality, it has existed throughout history. Do not misunderstand me – whilst I wish to stress that people struggling with self-harm should be loved and accepted, self-harm can be extremely dangerous and must be treated. If you are contemplating harming yourself, please take it from me – it is never the answer, and it will never benefit you. If you are considering self-harm, or have started to self-harm and wish to seek help with stopping, please, I beg you, call one of the helplines listed at the back of this book. You are not a disappointment or a let-down for suffering from it, and you are definitely, *definitely* not alone. There are millions of people around the world who self-harm as a coping mechanism, and whilst I don't believe it is an answer to anyone's problems, I do believe it is time we end this stigma of shame and embarrassment. Self-harming is common, and on the rise, especially in young adults. It should be talked about in schools so that self-harmers aren't made to feel *bizarre* or *stupid*, and far more support should be given in terms of school counselling. Self-harm shouldn't be swept under the rug as though it isn't a problem – it should be addressed as the rising problem that it is. In the meantime, however, please talk to a trained professional, who will not judge you or perceive you as *weak* or *stupid*. There are alternatives to starting this terribly addictive habit that can affect your health for the rest of your life. I believe in your ability to take these alternatives. All progress can only be made one day at a time. It will be tough, and temptations will be hard to avoid – but have faith in yourself and your own strengths. You are stronger than you think you are.

When it comes to having a friend who is self-harming, the advice I give can really only be loose-fitting. I do not know your friend, nor do I know their parents or their situation. In some circumstances, it might be best to tell your friend's parents – however, in others, that could make your friend's situation a whole lot worse, considering the stigma that still surrounds self-harming. What you absolutely *cannot* do under any circumstance is keep your friend's habit bottled up. Even if your friend has trusted you with their secret, it is not your burden to bear, and it is unfair of them to confide in you and make you feel as though you are helpless. Unless you are a trained professional – *you are not a trained professional!* You are not equipped to carry such a heavy burden, especially if you're of a young age. You cannot be expected to be the only person your friend has to turn to.

When I was fourteen, there was a girl I sometimes sat next to in class who didn't have a good home life. I will not divulge the specifics of this information out of decency, but one afternoon I noticed that the sleeve of her blazer had risen up. In the small gaps between the countless bracelets on her arms, I noticed those telltale red marks. As soon as she saw me looking, she pulled her sleeve down, looking away from me and furiously scribbling into her textbook. I said nothing, but from that moment on, I knew, and she knew that I knew. She never truly opened up to me about her situation, but one afternoon, I whispered to her, 'I just want you to know that if you ever want to talk, I'm here.'

She never did talk to me about it, but the pressure I felt to tell an adult about what she was doing was immense. However, I knew that if a teacher told her parents, there would be consequences for her. I felt as though any action I could take would hinder her, not help her. As far as I know, I was the only person in our school who knew her secret, and I felt powerless to help her. I know how it feels to carry a burden. It is always going to be a delicate situation, but you cannot allow yourself to carry someone else's secret if it is having an impact on their mental health. With the situation she was in, I feel fortunate that she didn't do something drastic. I cannot imagine how I would have coped knowing I could have done something to prevent that eventuality.

However – just because she got through her ordeal does not mean that everyone in a similar situation will. If you feel as though a friend might attempt to commit suicide, you absolutely must take action, and tell an adult, be it a parent or a teacher. The issue with self-harm is that a teacher, counsellor or doctor would most likely attempt to alert your friend's parents for safety reasons. Even if this doesn't have repercussions for your friend, your friend may feel as though you have betrayed them. Truly, it is a horrid situation to find yourself in, and I would beg you not to carry that burden alone. It is not your responsibility to keep such a big secret when it could potentially end in tragedy. Call one of the helplines at the back of this book and speak to a trained professional – ask what advice they would recommend. In the meantime, try to convince your friend to seek help, such as from a counsellor or doctor, or even a helpline if they are scared of their parents being alerted, and also let your friend know that you are there to support them if they need assistance in getting help.

Do not allow yourself to become your friend's sole confidante – it will take its toll on you as you feel more and more responsible for your friend's safety. Tell them that you are there for them whenever they need to talk, but urge them to take steps in order to stop self-harming. Invite them out on weekends to get them away from their home situation and keep them distracted from their thoughts, and don't get frustrated if they initially refuse to seek help. Telling someone about something that society shames you for whilst admitting to yourself that you have a problem is terrifying, and not something that can be done without a lot of mental preparation. Be there for them, promise to support them without judgement, and I wish you and your friend the best of luck.

I lost contact with my school friend a long time ago, but I do know that she is now studying to become a teacher, and spent some time travelling. She is always smiling in photos. She looks genuinely happy and healthy.

3

Life Is Unfair
(and so are people)

The Janis

Okay, important requirement for this section/life in general: have you watched the movie *Mean Girls*? You know, the 2004 classic, otherwise known as the greatest film of all time that defined a generation and provided us with a plethora of timeless catch-phrases such as, 'You go, Glen Coco!'

If you haven't, shut this book and go and watch it. Not just so that you get the reference in the heading of this section, but because your life will immediately become eight hundred per cent better.

Right, okay, you've watched it! Good stuff! Oh, Janis Ian, how I love you. You are a raven-haired, oversized-jacket-wearing, punk-loving comeback QUEEN. In every school you have the people who could fit into one of the many cliques from that film – the jocks, the nerds, the 'plastics'. I filled the role of Janis Ian. A black-haired, Green Day worshipping loudmouth who would give as good as she got – and I was just as unpopular as she was.

Throughout my secondary school, I was 'the goth', 'the emo', 'the dirty grunger' that even kids four years below me would shout abuse at in the corridor. My school life was plagued by bullying from kids in years above and below me, and I was often alone in class and at break. Combine my music taste and personality with the fact that I wasn't exactly all that particular about my personal hygiene (puberty was definitely working against me with the extra sweat and oils), as well as the fact that my family couldn't afford a spare school blazer so the one I owned often smelled pretty bad – I didn't exactly have my choice of friends. My later years at school were spent trying to fit in with groups of kids that were already cliques of their own, and none of them seemed particularly interested in allowing me in. Over the course of five years of secondary school, I attended a total of one party, one sleepover, zero after-school clubs and was a constant source of entertainment to a girl we'll call Rachel.

Rachel was our Regina George. Absolutely everyone that I knew in my school seemed terrified of her – she was physically imposing, and even the girls who would act as her 'backup' when she went to stalk her latest prey knew better than to get on her bad side. Rachel had no time for short, smelly 'goths'. Needless to say, I was Rachel's favourite target.

See, looking back at those times now, again with our good friend *hindsight*, it wasn't even what I looked like that drew Rachel to me, but the way that I handled her confrontation. As I said, as well as being comparable to Janis Ian in our shared fashion sense – army jackets and thick pencil eyeliner to boot – we also shared an instinct to fight back whenever someone said something nasty, no matter who they were. Whenever Rachel and her gaggle of geese came up to me hurling insults, I'd always tell them in no uncertain terms where to go – which never went down well. Rachel and her gang chased me down corridors on many an occasion, threatening to knock me out for something I'd said back to her – to which I'd finally respond by running away, locking myself in the toilets and crying. For most of my school life, it was like I was universally despised – no one wanted to hang around with the smelly, uncool goth/emo kid.

When I finally found a group of kids that didn't mind hanging around with me (older kids in the year above who had the same music taste that Rachel didn't dare to try fighting with – it's hard to pick on a big group of people who are older than you), I was left in peace. Over the years, I had tried changing my style so many times in an attempt to fit in – begging my dad to buy me the latest sports backpack, wearing a short skirt with tights in place of my usual baggy trousers and caking myself in fake tan (which, oh boy, went horribly wrong each and every time), but with this group of older kids, I felt accepted for who I truly was. When I went into the next year of school and my friends all moved on to college, I was devastated – alone and back to square one, hiding in the school library which Rachel and her friends would get kicked out of if they tried to start trouble. When I finally left school and discovered Rachel wasn't going to the same college as me, I breathed the biggest sigh of relief – at least I'd never go through bullying ever again . . . right?

High School Never Ends

Sad news – bullying doesn't magically stop when you leave school. I'm sorry. It may change form, but bullying exists in all walks of life – at home, school, college, university, work – and I found this out the hard way.

My first ever part-time job was in a shoe shop in my home town of Basildon. I was sixteen years old, the youngest you could be to get a job, and truth be told, I think I only got a callback because my CV was printed on light blue paper and stood out. (There's a top tip, direct from me to you.) My job entailed walking around the shop floor, replacing empty spaces on the shelves where shoes had been purchased with new, unsold shoes from the storeroom out back, asking customers if they needed help, measuring (and by default, touching – ew) the feet of strangers, manning the till, up-selling cheap, shitty shoe protector spray and trying to convince customers to sign up to our email newsletter so we could reach our daily target.

I could handle most parts of that job – but approaching customers who wanted to be left alone and asking if they'd give me their email address? Terrifying. I dreaded having to walk around handing out slips of paper with a form that asked for the stranger's full name, date of birth, home address, phone number, email address ... you can imagine the sheer hatred that appeared in the eyes of some customers, who just wanted to be left alone to try on a damn shoe.

On one quiet Sunday afternoon, towards the end of trading hours, I was standing by the till with my fellow part-timer Sam, who shared my hatred of handing out these stupid forms. It had been quiet all day, and almost every customer had seen through our bullshit – nobody wanted to get inundated with spam emails filled with crappy 'sale events'. As I was sharing my frustration at having to fill a quota for something nobody wanted, my supervisor 'Mel' walked over.

'Why aren't you out there getting emails from people?' she barked. Mel had only just been given the responsibility of running the shop on her own without needing a store manager present – something that she was desperately trying to prove was a good decision.

'We've tried, no customer here wants to do this stupid thing,' I snapped, having put up with her new sense of self-importance for hours and unable to handle her tone any longer.

'For fuck's sake, you're fucking useless,' she muttered, snatching the forms out of my fist and storming away from the till and on to the shop floor. In front of the customer service desk was a customer who had only walked into the store a few minutes before; someone we hadn't bothered yet.

'Excuse me, madam,' Mel said loudly, glaring over at me and Sam at the desk. Mel then proceeded to loudly bark the benefits of the email newsletter to this poor woman, who by the end of it looked so scared that she would've done anything to get away from being hounded.

Completed email form in hand, Mel strutted back over, slamming the paper down on the desk.

'There,' she snapped. 'Wasn't exactly hard, was it?' At this point, I watched the customer slowly put the shoes in her hand back on the shelf and quickly back out of the store.

'She'd only just walked in, Mel,' I replied angrily.

Bad idea. At this, Mel stepped forward, standing toe-to-toe with me, towering over me (that's probably obvious – everyone towers over me).

After a few heated words, I felt Mel's breath in my face. Her arms were out to the side, fists clenched, her cheeks bright red. *Am I about to get punched at work?* Fortunately, as I felt things were about to tip over, an older colleague came back from her break and separated us. I backed away into the staff room in tears – it certainly wasn't the only near-fight I'd had in my life, but this was in a working environment, somewhere I was supposed to feel safe.

I only stayed at the shoe shop for a couple of months after that incident, but right up until the day I quit, I could swear my locker was looking increasingly 'kicked in' and every so often my packed lunch seemed to go walkabout. Whatever was actually going on, all I know for sure is that Mel and I were never able to get on – and after I quit, we never spoke again.

Now, perhaps that's not *real bullying*, you may be saying. You annoyed her and talked back to a superior. Perhaps she was trying to prove that she could be trusted, and your incompetence was stressing her out. Well, it might just (definitely) be down to my personality, but I don't think I've had a 'real job' wherein I haven't felt hated by a manager – the worst example being when I worked in a fast food restaurant when I was seventeen to eighteen. I'll go into that story a little bit later.

Fact is, as the Bowling For Soup song says, *high school never ends*. There will always be gossiping, teasing, superiors that take advantage of you, superiors that treat you like dirt and, sometimes, confrontations. You know when people say it gets better?

They're wrong. It doesn't get better – *you* get better at dealing with whatever *it* is. So, as someone who has dealt with verbal and physical assaults through different stages of my life, what would I suggest in order to make it stop?

Making A (In) Difference

I'm fairly sure at this point I am obligated to give you the same spiel you've heard countless times before – tell a teacher, tell a parent, don't suffer in silence, count to ten and walk away. There you go. However, in my experience, there is a better way. Bear in mind it takes a while using this method, but in my experience, it does work about ninety-nine per cent of the time if you persevere. The trick is to be more stubborn than the bully and simply not *retaliate*. (Please remember that this is from my experience and every situation is different – above all else, you absolutely *must* tell someone if you are being bullied, even if you are scared of being a 'grass' or a 'snitch'. Make those at school, home or work sit up and listen to you. You can even contact the police if no one else is willing to help – your right to live without harassment is protected by law.)

Wow, I sound like I'm forty. Well, it's true, all right? There is an art to giving a bully nothing to work with. When I say nothing, I mean *nothing*. Zilch. Nada. There is one magic word that holds the key to beating your bully: *Okay*.

Ah, 'okay' is such a wonderful word! 'Okay' simmers so many arguments, because how can you fight someone that's in agreement with you? Just make sure that when you say the word 'okay', you're saying it in a neutral tone. Do not sound sad, or angry, or even really happy – you must remain completely indifferent to whatever someone has said to you. For example:

'Ugh, look, girls, it's the emo! Wash your hair, emo!'

'Okay.'

'Yeah, that's right, keep walking, minger! You reek of dog shit, does your mum smell like that too?'

'Probably.'

'Ha, she just admitted it! Her mum smells of dog shit! That's not very nice, is it?'

'No, I guess not.'

'Whatever, fuck off, weirdo.'

'Okay.'

All right, so at first you have to deal with a little hassle – remember that your bully is trying to get a rise out of you, stooping to levels such as trying to publicly humiliate you and insulting your family. When you give them nothing, they get desperate – and *look* desperate, too. At this point, your bully will probably tell you to 'fuck off', or something similar, and that's when you know that they have run out of steam. Keep walking, with your head high, and don't look back.

It may not be over after just one attempt – your bully may try again the next day with the same techniques, trying to embarrass you or insult you in a way that they think will hurt you. Remain calm, detach yourself from the insult – anger and hurt show on your face if you let their words get to you. Keep at it, day in, day out. Eventually, they *will* get bored. Simply 'walking away and counting to ten' (as we're so often told to do) and ignoring your bully will actually make them feel as though they're getting to you, and the insults may continue – or worse, escalate the situation into something more violent. If you find yourself alone at lunchtimes, as I often was, try to hang around places near members of staff. This, combined with the most neutral reactions you can offer, will help to shut your bully down very quickly.

Physical bullying is a little different – I would genuinely recommend walking away from someone trying to assault you. Whatever the kind of physical confrontation, I don't recommend trying to fight back. It is always best to back away if possible, even if you feel a bit cowardly. Do not do anything that could threaten your well-being. If someone is shoving you, or in any way trying to incite you to attack them back, walk quickly towards an area that has an authority figure to monitor the situation. Remember that any physical provocation is assault in the eyes of the law. If your school or workplace does not do anything to remedy the situation, call the police. At the very least, with witnesses or CCTV, the school/workplace will be forced to act, and your bully cautioned. Your school/workplace will be under a ton of pressure to prevent further attacks, and that bully isn't going to want another caution. If you fear that you are going to be physically attacked once you are alone, ensure that you can be escorted to where you need to be by someone else. Ask a friend to walk with you, or if you are at school/work, explain your fears to a teacher/colleague and get them to accompany you. Whilst physical bullying at a workplace is rare (and often rectified much sooner), it is sadly a lot more common in schools. If you tell a teacher that you fear that you will be physically assaulted once you are off school grounds, they should do everything in their power to help you avoid that situation. If you are being physically bullied, you absolutely must not stay silent. Sometimes a bully may threaten you with more violence if you tell an authority figure what they are doing, but that is because they want to get away with their bullying for as long as they can. Tell a parent, tell a teacher, or even tell the police if you believe it is necessary – whatever you do, do not suffer in silence.

Hopefully this last part goes without saying – if you see someone being bullied, do something. It doesn't matter if you don't know them. One of the quickest, simplest solutions to defusing a situation, whether it's bullying at school, or racist abuse on public transport, is to step in and strike up a conversation with the person being picked on – and completely ignore the bully's presence. Ask the victim if they're okay, talk about the weather, ask who their teacher is for geography, ask them if they'd like you to walk them to a classroom (or anywhere away from their attacker) – the person on the attack will have absolutely no idea what to do. Anything they shout in an attempt to regain control should be ignored entirely, and remember – bullies target people who are alone. By keeping their victim company, you are removing the bully's power. Make sure they are okay and then report the incident. If you do not feel comfortable getting this close to confrontation, immediately tell a member of staff what is happening. We all have a responsibility to reduce and eradicate bullying from any environment – remember that doing nothing is just as bad as being the bully.

4

Parental Controls

The Madonna

When I was sixteen, I got kicked out of my house.

Okay, maybe a little dramatic. I was threatened with being kicked out over the phone for a period of about ten minutes. Things sound better when they're sensationalised, all right? The Internet is seemingly ninety-nine per cent clickbait for a reason!

Let me set the scene: 13 November 2007, two days after my sixteenth birthday. A few days before, my friend Lucy had walked into our class with a nose piercing. *A nose piercing!* Immediately, without doubt or quarrel, she was the coolest person in our year.

'Yeah, I got it done in Southend,' she said, referring to the next town over. 'You're sixteen now, it's legal. You should get a piercing.'

Ah, young, impressionable Emma. I nodded eagerly, imagining

myself walking into class the next day with a Madonna piercing (a 'Madonna' is a stud above the right side of your lip, where Madonna's beauty mark is. All of the *coolest kids* on MySpace had one. Now that Lucy had a piercing and knew a good place, surely this was a sign that I should get one too?!).

After school was finished for the day, I texted my dad asking if I could go to Southend with some friends. The truth was, I was going alone, and straight to a piercing parlour. I knew exactly how my dad felt about facial piercings: 'Not under my roof.' My dad loathed facial piercings, always referring to them as 'ugly bits of metal in the face'. *Maybe when he sees that I have a Madonna piercing, he'll actually quite like it, and I won't be in trouble,* I foolishly thought, trying to convince myself this was a great idea. To my surprise, he agreed to let me go, under the impression I was finally hanging out with other people. My plan was in motion.

On the train ride to Southend, I started to feel nervous. I knew in the back of my mind exactly how my dad would react if I came home with a Madonna piercing. Not only was I getting a metal stud *in my face*, but I was also lying to him about what I was doing. I wasn't sure which action was going to make him angrier. It is worth noting that I wasn't doing any of this to spite him – it wasn't a case of teenage rebellion, as you might expect. My desperation to fit in at school by getting something 'cool' like a piercing simply overrode my logical thinking. Whilst I definitely knew it wouldn't go down well, I was holding on to a slither of hope that I'd created in my head that maybe – just maybe – he'd be okay with my choice once he saw it.

I'll save you the long, dramatic walk to the parlour – I got the piercing. It hurt. Have you ever heard your top layer of skin snap? It's gross. I walked out, nervous but triumphant – I finally had a Madonna piercing like the cool kids! I knew it would be better to call my dad and warn him about what I'd done rather than simply turn up at home with some metal in my face. *Perhaps in the time it takes to get home, he will have calmed down!* With a deep breath, I dialled my dad's number.

'Hey, pup!'

'Hey, Dad!'

'Had a good time in Southend?'

'Yeah, I got an upper lip piercing.'

Silence.

'What?'

'I got an upper lip piercing.'

Click. He'd hung up on me. *Oh God, it's worse than I thought*, and I quickened my pace back towards the train station. *I'm in for it now.*

Before I could conjure up any worst-case scenarios, my phone rang. It was my mum. Despite the fact that my parents had separated years before, they were still close friends – but Mum and I never phoned each other. Something serious was going down.

'Hello?'

'Emma, what have you done?'

'Uh, I got an upper lip piercing . . . why?'

'Right, get it taken out. Dad's about to throw your stuff out of the house.'

'What?!'

'Just get it taken out. I'll tell him you're getting it taken out and try and smooth things over.'

He was kicking me out? I'd known he was going to be upset, but never had I been kicked out of my house. I didn't dare try to phone him back – instead, I caught the train back to Basildon and went to our local parlour and got it taken out. (I know what you're thinking – if my home town had a piercing parlour, why didn't I just get the piercing done there? To this day, I don't have an answer for you. I just didn't have much common sense.)

When I got home, my face free of metal, I crept in, sheepishly walking into the living room where my dad was sitting. Clearly, my mum had worked her magic in calming him down. Instead of yelling, he simply ignored me as I said hello and went up to my room. I breathed a sigh of relief. He continued to be mad for a couple of days, communicating only in grunts, but eventually he began to forget the whole thing happened – up until now, that is. Sorry, Dad.

What's interesting about this story to me is that, a few years after it happened, I brought it up in conversation, and he told me why he was so angry. It wasn't that I'd got the piercing (although he still wasn't happy about it), it was because I'd gone behind his back and lied to him about going to Southend to get it done. If I had done the right thing and asked him, and he'd said no, I should've respected that – I was living under his roof, rent free, with meals cooked and clothes paid for, and lying about something was not the way to show gratitude.

So after reading a chapter about carving out your own path, and then one about doing as you're told – where is the line? When do we need to respect our parents' wishes, and when do we need to make our own decisions?

Who Do You Answer To?

As I said previously in this book, every so often in your life, there will come a time – whether it is far off in the future, soon, or even right now – when you will have no one to ask permission from, no one to ask an opinion from, and no one to answer to but yourself. This is why I always urge people not to follow in their parents' footsteps unless they are truly happy to do so – because one day, they won't be around, and you will be left with only what they wanted for you, and perhaps not what you wanted for yourself.

However, until that time comes, many of you reading this will have at least one parent that is trying to push you in a certain direction – whether that's forcing you to join after-school clubs, or telling you what to study, or that you need to work in the family business. Now, I'm not trying to tell you to rebel against your parents – they are people too, just like you, and I'll talk more about that later on in this chapter. However, it is important that, as you're beginning to find out who you truly are, you stay loyal to your own passions and aspirations. I didn't always do this growing up, in the form of not asking my parents if I could audition for school plays, and not studying the courses I would've enjoyed. There is a big difference, though, between living for yourself and disrespecting your parents. Sometimes all it takes is a little conversation. Communication is key.

Say that there is something you really want to do, such as join a club. Firstly, you have to communicate that to your parents. Sit them down, give them a flyer for the club if you have one, and tell them you really want to join. If they say yes, that's great!

However, if they say no, let's say because it's too far away, calmly ask for a compromise. Do you have a friend who is willing to join the club? Does that friend have a parent that could take the both of you? If not, would your parents be willing to let you join a club that is similar, but more local? Is there a way of promising to help around the house in exchange for a ride? If you're old enough to get a part-time job, could you go if you got a taxi there and back, or could you pay your parents to make the trip?

Sometimes there may be unavoidable reasons for why you can't go, such as the club being too expensive. In those scenarios, it's important to realise when something just cannot happen at this time in your life. Shouting and storming off will achieve nothing – and that goes for any dispute in your household. The way to get the best results from your parents is to treat them like humans, with their own lives and their own problems, all whilst trying to take care of the family. More on this later.

Let's go back to my Madonna piercing. Instead of lying to my dad about getting it done and then going behind his back to the next town before cowardly confessing what I'd done over the phone, I should have instead sat him down and asked him if I could get the piercing. He definitely would've said no, and I should've accepted that and not got it done, no matter how much I wanted it. The piercing wouldn't have affected my future, and doing something he was so against would've been disrespectful. No matter how cool I would've looked to my peers, it would never have been worth going behind my dad's back and damaging that relationship like I did.

However, there is a MASSIVE difference between a Madonna piercing and your entire future. If there is a certain dream you have, then you owe it to yourself to chase it down as hard as you can. This means doing things such as joining clubs, doing auditions, writing novel after novel, studying as hard as you can, volunteering at places simply for experience – whatever needs to be done to get closer to your dream job. Sometimes, your parents will not understand or appreciate what you want to do for the rest of your life. Perhaps they'll tell you it's unrealistic, and that you'd be safer working in an office than trying to be your own boss. Remember that, as hard as it is to hear it, your parents will only be saying that because they want to protect you. They want the best for you, and don't wish to see you as a 'starving artist' or unsuccessful and disheartened. However, if you work as hard as you can, and for as long as you can, you will begin to reap the rewards for your time and effort, and eventually your parents will be behind you every step of the way. It can be hard feeling as though you are doing something that is disappointing them in the short-term, but in time, they will realise that you have always been the master of your own destiny. No one on this planet really has that long – so you *have* to spend what little time you do have doing what you love. If that means going to university, or not going to university, or not joining the family business, or not doing a career your parents approve of, so be it. One day, you will be the only person you answer to. It will always be better to say, 'I wish I hadn't done that,' than, 'I wish I'd tried that.'

Parents Are People, Too

Oh great, you're thinking. I fight with my parents all the time and now Emma's defending them. Listen, I'll start off by saying that I don't know your parents. They may be lovely, or they may be complete arseholes who never listen to you. They could be wonderful to you and spoil you rotten, or physically and/or mentally abuse you. I do not, nor will I ever, know what hand you were dealt. However, I can guarantee one thing: your parents are human beings. Complex, troubled, stressed human beings, with thoughts, feelings and flaws. Once you begin to see them not as parents, but as adults, you can begin to change your relationship with them, and understand them on a completely different level. Once your parents become your friends, your life will be one hundred and ten per cent better.

A quick example: when I was twelve, after years of constant arguing, my mum and dad separated. My mum moved out of the family home, leaving just my dad and me. Whilst I had always been closer to my dad (he stayed home to look after me as a baby and my mum returned to work), their separation affected my relationship with my mum to the point of it becoming near non-existent. When she would come to visit me, I would stay up in my room, listening to loud rock and metal to drown out her voice from downstairs. I was angry and hurt and felt as though she had chosen to leave me, giving up on her marriage without a thought for how I felt.

Of course, that was never the case. Of course my mum had carefully considered my well-being every step of the way. Now, I have tried to write a more in-depth recollection of this time in my life, but I'm still finding it too difficult. My parents' separation was far more complex than any twelve-year-old could (or should) understand, no matter how much I tried to convince myself that I knew exactly what was going on.

I wish I could have seen the situation through the eyes of an adult, as I can now: my parents had been together for twenty years, money was tight, arguments were constant, their relationship had become increasingly strained and my mum simply couldn't cope with it any more. My mum was approaching forty and took solace in going out at night with her workmates and wasn't at home as often. She was at work five days a week in London, exhausted from the travelling and falling asleep on the sofa as soon as she got home, meaning my parents never had enough time to communicate, going to bed at different times and arguing every time I left the room. Both adults were unhappy, and separating was the best thing that could've happened for the both of them.

Once you begin to appreciate that your parents are adults with worries, vices, stresses and responsibilities, you can better understand them, and wanting to help them out becomes automatic. My family dynamic is completely different in the present day, thankfully – my parents are practically best friends, living only a few minutes away from each other, and my relationship with my mum is a lot better. I also have two half-siblings that I absolutely dote on. If you had asked me at the age of twelve what I thought my family would look like now, that definitely wouldn't be what I'd have imagined!

I feel it necessary to state here that whilst I am happy to say, 'Adults are people too! Talk to them!', absolutely nothing excuses emotional or physical abuse. If you are suffering at the hands of someone you should be able to trust, you must tell someone. There are helplines at the back of this book with people on the other end of the line who are there to help you.

Being 'only human' does not mean you should put up with any form of abuse.

Also it was only after moving out on my own for the first time at the age of twenty-two that I realised how little I helped around the house! I apologise to my dad almost weekly for never having done the washing-up or tidied up after myself – when there is more than one person in the house, each of you should do your share! I know that after a long day of school or work, the last thing you want to do is start doing chores – but your parents will have had a busy day, too, and doing just one extra task can help improve your relationship with them over time. It shouldn't be down to one person to do all of the cleaning. The same goes for money – when your parents say you can't have something, it can be easy to think that they're saying that to punish you, or because they're being selfish. The truth is, budgeting can be a bitch, and there may be bills you can't possibly account for. If one of your parents snaps at you for something seemingly small, they may be going through something unrelated that's weighing on their mind. Sometimes, simply asking, 'What's wrong, Mum/Dad?' can make the world of difference. Your parents can struggle, too – take it upon yourself to recognise when they need help and support, whether that's around the house or simply a listening ear. Recognise when the last thing they need is you pestering them about something that, all things considered, isn't that important, or you storming out of the room, shouting, 'THAT'S SO UNFAIR! I HATE YOU!' Sadly, this can be hard to do until you're an adult yourself and living on your own, by which time it's often too late.

Just remember this – putting yourself in the shoes of others can do wonders for a relationship. Communication and empathy are two of the most important skills that you can use to understand what someone else is going through. The moment I began to treat my parents as my peers as well as respecting them as my elders, they also became my friends – long gone are the years of shouting at each other and storming out of rooms. If ten years ago, someone had told me that this would be our dynamic, I wouldn't have believed them for a second.

5

Falling In Love
(and falling back out)

Knowing Your Rights

There is no right way to start a chapter about love. Love is a clusterfuck of emotions: sometimes happiness, often pain. I say that not as a cynic, but as someone who has experienced it all – crushes, unrequited love, long-term relationships, painful break-ups, amicable break-ups that have hurt even more over time – you name it, I've been there. If the world gave out sew-on patches for each emotionally-taxing experience related to love, my jacket would be completely covered in them. However, the point about love that I most want to communicate to you is that you have many rights that you should feel no shame in exercising:

- You have the right to feel comfortable and happy in every scenario, be that physically or emotionally.

- You have the right to say no to anything you do not feel comfortable with.

- You have the right to have your feelings heard and respected.

- You have the right to remain *you*, with every quirky personality trait, every strange hobby and any faith you may have.

- You have the right to be in a relationship without emotional manipulation or physical and/or sexual abuse.

- You have the right to walk away from any relationship that is unhealthy.

- You have the right not to feel stupid for having feelings for someone who does not reciprocate them.

- You have the right not to like someone back without being insulted, blackmailed or threatened.

- You have the right not to be taken advantage of by someone you have a crush on or are in love with.

❥ You have the right to be respected as a human being in a relationship.

❥ You have the right to grieve when a relationship ends.

❥ You have the right to love yourself *at least* as much as you love someone else, if not more.

Feeling Crushed

Firstly, my apologies to those who do not experience crushes. I am aware of how many times those who fall on the asexual spectrum must be told each and every day, 'Perhaps you just haven't found the right person yet! You will!' and it is most certainly not my intention to make anyone feel excluded from this book. However – crushes are ruddy horrible, and whilst I'm sure the grass is always greener, I have wished many times throughout my life to be able to rip out the part of my brain responsible for them. They are often long, drawn-out and emotionally exhausting, and if I could go through the rest of my life never having another one, I'd be okay with it.

Some emotions that I have experienced from having a crush:

❥ Like you're floating on air. Suddenly you can imagine a plethora of scenarios involving you and your new interest, such as them confessing how they like you back, your first kiss, your first . . . well, you know. It depends on how vivid your imagination is. Mine is vivid.

❥ Like your heart is being torn in two when things don't work out the way you'd planned. Heartbreak can genuinely give you physical feelings of illness. This happened to me a little while back. I'll talk about that in a moment.

❥ Anger, if you fell for someone who is actually a horrible twit and realising you spent months of your life trying to justify to yourself that they were secretly lovable and *changeable* when you knew deep down that your efforts would be futile.

❥ Jealousy, of the person they're dating or crushing on that isn't you. By the way, as a side-note, as tempting as it may be to act out of selfishness and try to ruin your crush's current relationship, don't do it. I'll talk about that later, too.

Overall, crushes can make you feel incredible. The human body completely transforms when it experiences feelings of love. Love can also lead you to feeling awful, make you act in a way that you never imagined you would and make you wish you'd never met that perfect, wonderful, absolutely diabolical human. Every feeling you experience whilst in love, whether positive or negative, is amplified to the extreme. And guess what? All those feelings are valid. Time for some stories.

Technically, my first crush was Charlie Simpson, a member of the pop band Busted. I was twelve years old and madly, madly in love, with the band's albums on repeat, posters of him all over my walls, and daydreams of our future together (once we met and fell in love at first sight, of course). Look, I'm not going to sit here and write that crushes on celebrities are stupid (I've got my list. Wrestlers, mostly), but this one was definitely born from the sudden emergence of hormones and not something I ever wish to bring up to Charlie, who is now someone I know quite well on a personal level. Fortunately, I don't think this book is his kinda thing. Let's just not tell him.

Instead, let's talk about my first actual crush on a human being that I knew in the 'real world'. We'll call him 'Harry'. I was thirteen, and Harry was in my year at school, albeit not in any of my classes, and he was my absolute dream boy. Somehow, I managed to weasel my way into his friendship group, and we began hanging out at lunchtimes in the school library. The library was his gang's usual hangout spot, and soon, every one of my lunchtimes was spent at the same table with the usual people – myself, Harry, and three or four of his friends. I still remember the day I got Harry's phone number – it was such a victory to me, and yet I never actually texted him because I was too nervous!

Unfortunately, it was no secret how much I liked Harry. I never have been – nor will I ever be – the queen of subtlety. When I have a crush on someone, they know. Any time Harry addressed me, I would blush a bright beetroot red, my words stumbling over one another as I tried to respond to his acknowledgement of my presence. My friends knew, his friends knew, and Harry *definitely* knew.

Unfortunately for me, Harry didn't like me back. This 'unrequited love' thing seems to be a running theme in my life, and sadly, is probably one of the only consistent things about me.

When your crush doesn't like you back, you go through a few trains of thought:

Maybe if I keep hanging around with him, he'll see that we're perfect together!

Perhaps if I do nice things for him, he'll fall for me . . .

You know what, today I'm just going to ignore him. Oh, who am I kidding . . . ?

Before I knew it, I found myself deep in the 'friend zone'. We could have many discussions here about whether or not the 'friend zone' exists or whether it's simply a social construct for someone acting bitter about being rejected, but for simplicity's sake, you all know what the 'friend zone' is, and so that's how I'm going to put it. I was madly 'in love' with Harry, would have done anything for him, and was waiting with bated breath each day for when he'd finally ask, 'Emma . . . will you be my girlfriend?'

I was going to leave this part out, because it involves some . . . dubious activity by two thirteen-year-olds, but I made a pledge to tell the whole truth in this book. There was one lunchtime that was different to all the others. I entered the school library, as per usual, and walked up the stairs to our table – *as per usual* – and sat down next to Harry. For a while, everything seemed normal – the same banter, the same packed lunches, the same feeling of my heart trying to thump its way out of my chest – until I felt a hand on my leg.

Now, it's safe to say that the thought of sex was quite a way off at this point – all the things that many teenagers with hormones do weren't even on my radar – but Harry's warm hand on my leg made me feel something that wasn't just butterflies in my stomach. I was young (*too* young), I thought I was in love, and I thought this was Harry showing affection for me, so I let him continue. Now, I think it's important to note that this was all *above clothes* – but it didn't stop me from putting my hand on his leg in return. Slowly, underneath the table in the library, unbeknownst to our friends around us, our hands moved up each other's legs towards . . . more private areas. Nothing really happened except our hands sort of . . . moving, I guess. Almost as soon as it started, it stopped. The lunch bell rang and Harry stood up, grabbing his bag (and probably tugging his shirt down a bit. I can't remember). At the time, I felt overjoyed. Did this mean Harry liked me? That he was attracted to me?!

Thankfully (although I wasn't saying so at the time), it never happened again. It's only really as I'm writing this that I realise how angry I still am at Harry for doing what he did. I have no doubt that in the decade that has passed, he has grown to be a kind, respectful person towards women, but before this incident, I had never linked my feelings for someone to doing things of a sexual nature. After that experience, at the age of thirteen, I did. I'm not sure it's fair to blame him retroactively, but knowing that he was aware of how I felt and actively chose to do what he did that lunchtime makes me want to reiterate one of the points I made earlier: You have the right not to be taken advantage of by someone you have a crush on or are in love with.

I'll spare you the rest – the perfect, beautiful relationship between us that I'd spent countless nights imagining never blossomed. Harry got a girlfriend, who I hated simply because she had what I wanted (which is no reason to hate someone, by the way – don't blame someone for making your crush happy). Eventually, my feelings for Harry faded, and we lost contact after we left school – that is, until at the age of twenty-three I bumped into him in London where he was working. I don't personally believe in *coincidence*, and to me this 'chance meeting' was destined to happen. I was supposed to see him there, equipped with far more confidence than I'd had ten years earlier (I was hotter, too), and get that little bit of closure on the time I'd spent pining for him. We spoke for a while, and I walked away graciously with my head held high. It wasn't a case of feeling smug – he was probably an entirely different person to the one I fell for – but more a way of telling myself: *You are not the weak person you once were.*

I really hate it when people older than me say, 'When I was your age . . . ' so please don't think I'm trying to be 'that guy', but when you're a teenager, with hormones raging (wow, I sound forty), crushes can be torture if they're not reciprocated, especially if you're a bit of a deep-feeling being like myself. I spent many hours of that time in my life daydreaming about Harry in my classes, thinking of what our first kiss would be like, immaturely wishing he'd break up with his oh-so-perfect girlfriend when he realised how much *better* I was . . . it was a cycle of getting my hopes up and then having them dashed, multiple times a day. In the end, I was practically torturing myself. It's completely normal (as is not having crushes at all, by the way! Asexuality is a hundred per cent valid, *obviously*) to go through the motions of getting addicted to the butterflies, even if it leads you to ask what you need to change about yourself – but my advice would be if you know someone you like doesn't like you back, try your hardest to walk away. If they're your friend, and you don't want to ruin that friendship, perhaps try to create a little distance until your feelings have faded – but make sure that you're staying in contact with them for the right reasons. I know it's hard. If the person you're madly in love with is taken, or simply isn't interested, respect that. Do not think that simply doing nice things (or favours of an . . . adult nature) will change your situation – and do not try to break up a relationship for your own selfish gain. Time for the second story, then . . .

Fast forward a few years. I'm now sixteen years old, fresh into college and fresh out of my first 'real' relationship that had lasted almost a year, suddenly surrounded by hundreds of new faces. Basically, I'm on the rebound. I'm hurt, I'm looking for comfort. Word to the wise – if you have a broken heart, don't immediately look for relief in someone else. Take time out to heal, love your-self and accept that you cannot love someone fully until you have processed that break-up. Being single is not the end of the world.

As well as studying English, maths and politics, I also chose to study ICT (computing, for those who don't call it that) and it was here that I met a boy called . . . let's go with 'Arnold'. Arnold was a bassist in a band, shy and sweet, with beautiful eyes and a smile that could melt your heart. He was assigned the seat next to mine, and over the next few weeks, we got talking. I began to realise that Arnold was cute as heck, and I was pretty sure he liked me back. Sweet!

Except Arnold had a girlfriend.

I'm sure you can predict where this is going. I was sixteen, and at that time in my life, I wasn't mature enough to see the bigger picture and empathise with others very well – I wanted Arnie all to myself. Arnold was madly in love with a girl called 'Beatrice' who he had been seeing for about two years, but he was easily swayed. I think it goes without saying, but looking back at it now, I obviously regret this entire situation. Sixteen-year-old Emma does not reflect twenty-five-year-old Emma, and I'm sure thirty-four-year-old me will think I'm an idiot for the things I do now, too.

Eventually, after several weeks of getting to know each other, many heart-eye glances exchanged and texts flying back and forth, Arnold and I agreed to hang out one weekend. We went to the annual festival in my home town, and ended up holding hands and eventually shared a kiss. As selfish as I was, and as fast as my heart was pounding, I remember the immediate guilt I felt for Beatrice, who was probably sitting at home miles away and had no idea what had just happened. I suddenly felt awful. Beatrice went to the same college as Arnold and I, and although I didn't know her all that well, the sudden realisation of how much this was going to hurt her sank in. To Arnold's credit, he told her straight away – and sadly, it led to them breaking up. Suddenly, my feelings of happiness evaporated and were replaced by the realisation that I was the reason Beatrice was now going through something so awful, feeling betrayed and abandoned so cruelly. Yes, Arnold most certainly played his part – 'it takes two to tango', as they say – but I knew I had to accept my share of the responsibility. Arnold and I ended up trying to date, but the guilt we both felt for the way that we had got together took its toll, and we only lasted a couple of weeks. A two-year relationship, ruined through fleeting feelings of lust – we were both to blame, and we knew it.

Of course, with college being an education facility with hundreds of teenagers who all knew each other in some capacity, word got around very quickly about what we had done. Although Arnold got off pretty lightly with his peers, I most certainly didn't. Girls who would usually say hello at lunchtime now scowled at me, surrounding Beatrice like bodyguards ready to pounce on me if I so much as looked at her. I was completely cut off from the few friends I had managed to make in those first short weeks of college, and once Arnold and I had broken up, that reputation stayed with me for the entirety of my first year. Needless to say, Beatrice had a few choice words for me when I eventually tried to apologise, and I don't blame her in the slightest. I would absolutely understand if she still thinks of me with disdain – even though she and Arnold ended up reuniting and have been together ever since. It's been almost ten years since it happened, and I still feel guilty for being their 'blip'.

A word to the wise: if you are tempted to do what I did, please don't. Don't ruin someone else's happiness to find your own. If the person you like is happy in a relationship, be happy *for* them. If you think the person you like is unhappy in a relationship, let them discover that for themself, in their own time and on their own terms – you could actually be very wrong. I know it can be hard seeing everything you want right in front of you, just out of reach, but the feelings of guilt you end up having, in addition to the consequences of your actions, will cancel out any joy you get from stealing your crush away. Start a relationship in the right way – if it's tainted from the start, that's how it will probably continue. If you 'won' someone through making them cheat, can you ever truly trust that they won't do the same again, only to you? That isn't to say all relationships that start out this way are doomed – but for me personally, the hurt you end up causing completely ruins that feeling of victory when that dream person is led astray.

Let me tell you though, and I'm sorry for getting a bit too real here – the heartbreak never gets easier. In the time since, I've had crushes that have ended in disaster (again, don't date your band-mates!), crushes that have been reciprocated and blossomed into long, happy relationships, and again gone through the motions of having a crush on someone who already had a girlfriend. It hurt at thirteen, and it hurt again at twenty-four. The only real thing that changes is your level of naivety – last year, when I found out my then-crush was already taken, I knew the sort of pain I was in for, because on paper he seemed perfect. Funny and cute, with a love of wrestling? Count me in. Looking back, I was definitely still hurting from the break-up of my longest-ever relationship, and it was definitely too soon in my personal healing process to be looking for someone new. However, things moved quickly. Pretty soon, we were sliding into each other's DMs (wow, that reference is going to date this book, isn't it?) and talking every day. Twitter messages evolved into texts, and pretty soon, I was hooked. Now and again, he would mention a 'lady', but because of how casual he seemed about her, and how deep our conversations would get, I was under the impression that he was just sort of 'seeing' someone. Even at twenty-four you can be as naive as you choose to be. I should have walked away the second I heard another girl's name, but by the time I began to wonder how involved they really were, I was in too deep, and I found myself sitting on a chair next to him and some of his friends in a bar halfway across the country, overwhelmingly smitten and drunk enough to pour my heart out.

After an awkward, drunken conversation, I ended up asking the question I knew I should have asked at the start, back in the Twitter DMs:

'How long have you been with your girlfriend, anyway?'

'About two years.'

You know those vertical-drop rides at awful amusement parks, where you slowly rise to the top and, after an excruciating pause, you're dropped at full speed to the floor, and your stomach feels like it's going to come out of either your mouth or your butt? That's exactly how I felt. Except for a whispered, 'Right . . . ' no words could leave my mouth. A few moments later, the 'perfect' guy, who had only really mentioned a girl in passing to the point where I thought they'd been on a couple of dates, made an excuse to leave, and I was left in the bar with a handful of his friends. As soon as I said goodbye to him, I remember physically falling to my knees and crumpling into a drunken ball of tears (I am a dramatic drunk), sobbing as one of his female friends rushed over to comfort me, furious at how he'd strung me along.

It's odd to me now that I knew on the drive up to see him

that I would probably have to have this conversation, and yet I'd somehow fooled myself into thinking that I was mentally prepared for it. Needless to say, the long drive back home was horrible. This is one of the few instances that I can say I've experienced the physical symptoms of heartbreak. The morning after that awful conversation, I just felt ... not anything like my usual self, and it wasn't related to the hangover. My body ached, my mind was working at limited capacity, and I just felt generally awful. Okay, that *does* sound like a hangover, but I promise you it was different. I don't know how else to describe it, but my friend who had come with me explained it in a way I've never forgotten – when you're in love, your brain forms connections that produce happy hormones when you think about that person. When you experience heartbreak, your brain has to destroy those links. Listen, I'll level with you, I don't know if that's scientifically proven. I suppose I could look it up, but the imagery of that is so compelling to me that I sort of don't want to find out. The thought of being physically tied to someone and having to physically detach yourself when the time comes – it's an awful, painful process, but strangely beautiful, too. However, if I was asked if I wanted to voluntarily experience that feeling again, I think I'd just laugh at you.

Let's get to the moral of the story. My advice to you is simply that if your crush mentions having a girlfriend or boyfriend but continues to play up to your affections – they're stringing you along. Whether or not you choose to distance yourself from them or not is down to you, but simply be aware that their relationship status isn't likely to change, regardless of what you buy them, what favours you do for them, and no matter how much you change yourself for them. Unrequited love is hard, and only time can get you through it – but by dedicating your time to friends and family, not saying yes to every little favour and using creative outlets such as art or songwriting, you'll get through it! Wait for someone who loves you back, openly and honestly, and who ultimately will respect you and not use your feelings to get something they want, and wait for a love where nobody around the two of you will feel abandoned or betrayed. Those relationships are the ones truly worth holding out for.

Breaking Up

Want to know what's worse than wanting someone and not having them? Having someone and then losing them. Whether it ends in a screaming match or you both hugging it out, a break-up is absolutely devastating because it signifies a state of change you could never have prepared yourself for. Change is scary, regardless of how it happens. Before I talk about a few of my break-ups, I want to state this: if you're going through a break-up, no matter what it was over, love yourself. Be kind to yourself. Allow yourself to grieve (yes, a break-up is still a loss, and you *will* go through a grieving process similar to that of mourning a death) and don't rush into something else in an attempt to get over it. The only thing that will heal you is time. 'They' ('they' say a lot of things, don't 'they'?) say that it can take up to a third of the time you were dating someone to fully get over them, sometimes longer. Do not look for someone to fill that sudden void – love yourself again before trying to love another.

My first relationship started and ended when I was sixteen years old. His name was Ben, and we were together for ten months back in 2007–2008. I truly (foolishly) thought I'd found *the one*. We'd met on MySpace, as many kids did *back in the day* – and through a couple of black-and-white photos of him performing in his pop-punk band on stage, I developed the *biggest* crush on him. Ben was two years older than me, and cooler than any other boy I'd fancied – in my mind, he was the *dream boy*. Somehow, after hundreds of instant messages sent back and forth between us, he agreed to go on a date with me. He turned up to that first date an hour late, but later on we ended up hanging out at the top of a massive hill, where we ended up kissing. *Yes!*

After returning home from our successful first date, I logged on to MySpace, only to see a message from him:

> hey it was fun hanging out, gotta be honest with u though i felt like it sort of lacked something. you just didn't have the wow factor. But yh lets chat later x

Saying that I didn't have the 'wow factor' ... *ouch*. Looking back, that probably should have been a red flag. Ben had also just been dumped by a girl he really liked, but in my mind, he was still the *dream boy*, and I was sure I could show him just how great I was. After agreeing to go on a second date, he asked me to be his girlfriend. In retrospect, I probably should have realised he'd pretty much just settled for something to distract him from his last break-up, or even worse, to make his ex feel jealous – ah, youth.

Ben and I had been together for almost a year when I went with him, his sister and his best friend to a forest getaway resort, and after a couple of days in each other's constant company, we began to argue. As it turns out, we were totally incompatible with each other for more than a few hours at a time. Before the holiday, we'd only really hung around with one another for a few hours each Saturday at his parents' house. Being around each other every hour of every day for more than a week was something that we'd never done before, and these arguments that we had on this holiday ended up getting so bad that eventually he was sleeping on the sofa in the cabin instead of in our double bed, and any conversation between us during the day was strained at best.

As soon as we were back from the holiday, I met up with him and suggested that we break up. Immediately the words left my mouth, I regretted them – was I really going to throw away our otherwise perfect relationship over a couple of bad weeks? To my surprise, though, Ben seemed *more* than happy for us to split up. I later found out through 'Arnold' (remember him?) that Ben had referred to me as a 'rebound that went wrong' to his friends. However, despite the sadness I felt for our failed relationship, and his friends shouting abuse at me whenever I walked past them, nothing compared to the heartbreak I felt when he fell for someone else almost immediately.

A couple of weeks after Ben and I broke up, I started my first year of college. Of course, I had chosen the college that he was already attending, and I began to regret my decision almost immediately. Don't make important decisions based solely on love, kids! Whenever I passed Ben in the hallways, my heart would begin to pound, and yet we simply looked away from each other, not even saying hello. Someone I cared so much about was becoming a stranger, and after I suggested we meet in private and asked if he wanted to give it another go, he coldly shut me down.

A few weeks pass by, and I'm walking down the hallway towards another class when suddenly, out of a door in front of me, comes Ben – holding hands with a girl from my year, 'Jasmine'. Jasmine was a girl who had a much cooler music taste, long, flowing blonde hair and a beautiful face – and I was distraught. For the next thirty seconds, I had to walk behind Ben and his new girlfriend holding hands, seemingly so in love that nothing could tear them away from each other. I quickly dived into the nearest bathroom and cried my eyes out.

The next few weeks of feeling replaced were unbearable, but in time it became less painful. Eventually I found a new group of people to hang out with at lunchtime, away from where Ben and Jasmine sat making out, and as my feelings for Ben faded, they were replaced with feelings for Arnold. Those couple of months were extremely confusing, upsetting and filled with gossip and drama – and being only sixteen, with emotions running wild, coursework stress already mounting as well as personal family drama going on, I felt completely out of my depth. At times, I felt as though things would never get better, that my life would always be full of this sadness and confusion and I would regret breaking up with Ben for ever. Funnily enough, almost ten years on, I'm sitting here laughing as I write this. Not that my feelings then weren't valid, but the knowledge that hard times are always temporary has never been clearer than it is right now.

This story definitely has an interesting ending, though. Ben and Jasmine stayed together for a few more years, and I lost contact with him after I left college – that is, until 2013, when Ben discovered that I made YouTube videos that were becoming pretty successful. When he messaged me out of the blue asking to meet up with him for a coffee, I agreed, mostly for a bit of closure, and admittedly because I can be a bitter old fool at times, and I was feeling a bit smug that the musician *dream boy* from years ago was suddenly trying to worm his way back in with me. We met up in my town, which he'd never agreed to during our relationship. By this point, my feelings for him had obviously completely died, but his had come surging back – and he'd even begun to distance himself from Jasmine. Was it because I was 'cool' now? Was it because suddenly, through hard work, I was achieving all of the things he and his band wanted?

Little did he know that, in those short years, Jasmine and I had become good friends after she and Ben began to experience problems, and we were messaging back and forth about Ben's shitty behaviour. Turns out Jasmine was still (just about) dating Ben, even though Ben clearly had other intentions with our coffee hangout. I told Ben in no uncertain terms what I thought of his behaviour once I found out, and Jasmine broke up with him and never spoke to him again. Sometimes we still laugh at the fact that we both somehow put up with his behaviour (not to mention his lack of personal hygiene – you gotta scrub everywhere, boys). Time has healed us both. However, this isn't the only story involving Jasmine in this book – remember her name.

And, Ben, if you're reading this, part of me hopes you've learned a thing or two about the way you treat women. I sincerely hope that with time, you have become a better human. Judging from what I've heard on the gossip mill, though, you haven't. Please stop trying to friend request me on every social media website you can find. I'm not interested in helping your new band out. I hope you find happiness as Jasmine and I both have without you.

So, It's Over

Now, without trying to go all *when I was your age* on you, it's interesting to me that over the course of my life, I have said 'I love you' to many people I've dated, but have only been in love once. That's not to say I *lied* to the other people I was with – simply that I thought I knew what love was, right up until I actually found it. Let me tell you, if you haven't already experienced it, being *in love* with someone is entirely different to simply being happy when you're around someone. Breaking up with someone you really care about is still hard – but losing the one person I truly loved was the worst emotional pain I have ever experienced. Wow, how dramatic. That said, after being *in love*, which is what we're all told as kids is what we're ultimately searching for, let me state a few truths about love – if not for you, then definitely for myself. I'll try not to get too deep:

> ⚡ You can be in love and still be unhappy.
>
> ⚡ Love cannot solve every single problem you have.
>
> ⚡ You can definitely be angry at someone you love.
>
> ⚡ It is okay not to see the person you love as completely perfect.
>
> ⚡ The movie of your life doesn't end once you find love.

> ⚡ Love is not an emotion, but an emotional state that can take years to come out of.
>
> ⚡ Staying friends with someone you're in love with makes losing them harder.

Up until recently, I'd never had a break-up where the two of us managed to stay friends. It was simply too difficult – questions and bitter remarks would always arise, and things would get awkward. The relationship between myself and the bassist from my first band actually ended with us yelling at each other and both of us writing songs about each other . However, in 2016, my longest, most serious relationship ever had come to an end. I don't want to go into this too much, as my ex and I both make videos online, and our relationship was very public, which of course meant that our break-up was, too. The thing is, nothing bad actually happened between us – sometimes communication doesn't have to break down to the point of screaming and shouting. Our relationship simply ran its course. We both began putting most of our time and energy into our careers, and our relationship ultimately paid the price. We worked hard to remain close friends, but, as I found out, staying friends with someone you still love can sometimes be harder than drawing a line under it all and never speaking to them again.

The problem with staying friends with an ex is that, during your relationship, your brain will associate that person with happiness, and whenever you're sad, your brain will crave any source of happiness hormones it remembers. Imagine feeling sad over a break-up and as though the only thing that can make the sadness go away is confiding in the person that you're feeling sad over! In my situation, the first few months of trying to hang out with my ex as a friend confused my brain and tore my heart in two. *Why aren't we cuddling him?* my brain would ask, though I knew I couldn't if I didn't want to make him uncomfortable. Seeing him sleeping in a separate bed in my hotel room at a YouTube convention was so odd, and so hard. However, our friend Father Time heals those wounds, too. Whilst I think I will always care for my ex and want the very best for him, I am finally able to hang out with him now without the longing to hold his hand. Your brain is in a constant state of rewiring itself, changing your thoughts and opinions on everyone and everything you know. Whether you remain friends with an ex or not, your brain has to go through a healing process – rebounding into a new relationship might create new links in your brain, but it won't help break the old links any faster. With that all said, regardless of whether you remain amicable or not, here are a few things about breaking up:

- Give yourself time. You will cry. You will be upset. You will be angry. Those feelings will pass.

- Do not torture yourself with questions like: What if we hadn't broken up? Would things have been different if I hadn't done this or that? Unanswerable questions solve nothing, and only lead to feelings of guilt and self-doubt.

❧ You may feel as though you'll never love again, but I promise you that you will. Your heart and mind will mend, and you will regain the ability to love and trust someone else. It may take weeks, months or even years. Do not pressure yourself or force yourself to get into anything you're uncomfortable with. The right kind of love is worth waiting for.

❧ Don't bitch about your ex. No, really, don't. It does no good to sling mud. It may feel good in the short-term bitching to your friends about the bad things your ex would do, or insulting your ex's new love interest, or talking trash about his or her body, but those things will inevitably get back to your ex, which will hurt them (do you really want that? Even if they hurt you first?), or could even lead to them retaliating with their own gossip and rumours. You want the hurt done and out of the way as fast as possible. Starting unnecessary fights will prolong the pain.

❧ If your ex asks if the two of you can get back together, think long and hard, and do not make any decisions in haste. Rationally remember why it ended in the first place, and ask yourself if you are truly compatible. Additionally, if you ask your ex if the two of you can get back together and they say no, respect that! You can't make someone fall back in love with you. Do not make up lies or try to make them pity you and especially don't emotionally blackmail them! Absolutely nobody likes being rejected, but always be kind and respectful, even if it ended badly.

- Don't ask for gifts back. That's shitty. Similarly, if you have something of theirs that wasn't given to you as a gift, and they ask for it back, be decent and return it to them. Don't keep it out of spite in order to cause them grief. If you keep communication open and honest, this exchange shouldn't be too much of a problem.

- Change other aspects of your life now that your relationship status has changed! This is the perfect time to make new friends, take up new hobbies, go to the festival you always wanted to go to – new things will help to take your mind off the heartbreak. Our minds always focus on the saddest parts of our lives when we are idle, and if you suddenly find yourself alone a lot more often, you'll end up stuck in a cycle of remorse as you compare your current state to the time when you felt happier.

 Forgive yourself. Whether your relationship
 ended due to something you did, or whether your
 ex did something to hurt you, or whether the
 relationship simply ran its course, it wasn't meant
 to be at that moment in time. If things ended,
 you simply weren't compatible. Of course, if you
 think you can work through your issues, and
 the relationship's definitely right for both of you,
 then that's great – but absolutely take the time to
 decide whether it's for the best or whether you're
 simply following an irrational, broken heart. Be
 kind to yourself. Allow yourself to feel upset.
 Don't listen to the friends who tell you to 'just
 get over it'. They are not you, and haven't walked
 in your shoes. It is human to feel heartbroken. A
 heart that hurts is a heart that works.

6

Sex
(or lack thereof)

The Big 'S'

Man, I don't know how to start this chapter. Isn't it odd how we know that sex is taboo to discuss, and that we all so desperately want to break that taboo, but still find it difficult to talk about? Well, at least I do. I suppose I'll start off by saying that if you're reading this and you're either my mother or my father, you can *absolutely* skip this chapter. I *definitely* won't mind. You see, I've done things I'm not proud of and I've never told you, and I'm still not sure that I want you to find out. However, I promised myself that this book would tell the whole truth, or it wouldn't exist at all, so here's the first big confession . . .

I started 'fooling around' when I was thirteen. After that under-table experience with 'Harry', the world of sex suddenly entered my life like a freight train. What was going on *down there*?

Slowly, and then all at once, I transformed from an innocent girl who only cared about her favourite boy bands in a cute way into a teenager who was developing into more of an adult every day, surrounded by peers that were discovering sexuality in their own ways and bragging about sexual acts they were supposedly doing with other boys and girls. I was young, immature, and suddenly led by my hormones, despite having had the talk about periods with my mum only a couple of years earlier. After the feelings I had for Harry began to fade, a boy called 'William' asked me out. It was a typical school playground romance – I think his friend was the one who came up to me and asked if I wanted to 'go out' with him, and within a week, we were grossing out all of our friends by making out every lunchtime. We said 'I love you' after two days, and he proposed after a week. Yes, a week. Truly a love to last throughout the ages, ladies and gentlemen.

After two weeks of constant hand-holding and ... I don't know, planning our future, I guess, I plucked up the courage to ask my dad if William could come back to our house after school. To my surprise, my dad agreed, probably thinking we'd just listen to CDs in my bedroom. However, I definitely had other plans. You see, by this point, I was surrounded by friends bragging about having sex, and I had a burning desire to be a part of the world they were talking about. I felt as though I was the only person in my year who wasn't having sex, and I was going to change that.

Now, fortunately – *very* fortunately – after suggesting to William in my bedroom that we do a lot more than make out, he completely shut down the idea, saying he wasn't ready. Damn well bloody good for you, William, and thank you for doing that (it probably also had something to do with an ex-Army man who was very protective of his daughter sitting downstairs), because, looking back, I definitely wasn't ready for sex either. However, after kissing for a while, we did end up doing some more . . . adult things. It wasn't 'all the way', but it was pretty much everything else – until we heard footsteps. Very quickly, school trousers were being hoisted back up, and I *literally leapt into my cupboard* so that my dad wouldn't see me getting dressed again. I'm making this sound quite funny, but at the time I felt nothing but dread as my dad opened my bedroom door to see a boy looking quite flustered and me behind my cupboard door trying to do my trousers back up. Instantly envisioning the (probably correct) situation, my dad stormed straight back out, slamming the door, and I truly wanted the ground to swallow me up. To this day, I have never felt more mortified. Ashamed and dreading the trouble I was clearly going to be in, I rushed to the bathroom and threw up. That, my friends, is the story of my first sexual encounter. How romantic.

After I sheepishly returned from walking William to the bus stop by my house, I fully expected my dad to explode at me in a full-blown rage. What I got was worse – a look of disappointment and total silence. I quickly ran back up to my bedroom and started crying. Was the rush to 'get it over with' and tell my peers that I was cool like them really worth it? It was then that I realised that I was completely out of my depth, and I hadn't been emotionally ready or mature enough for what we'd done. After a few hours, I went downstairs – even being shouted at was better than being ignored. This time, my dad did something that still surprises me to this day when I think about it. He calmly sat me down and said, 'Emma, boys your age are idiots. Tomorrow, everyone is going to know what you were doing. They're going to think some horrible things about you now. Be prepared for that.'

That was it. No name-calling or shaming, no yelling at me for being stupid – just a piece of advice from a clearly disappointed man. And do you know what? He was right. Everyone *did* find out the next day at school. 'William' had told a couple of friends, who had gone on to seemingly tell everyone and their dog. Only, what we'd done wasn't met with praise or celebration from my friends like it was with his – everyone I spoke to thought it was gross. That was when I realised that all of the kids that were bragging about what they'd done with eighteen-year-olds were lying. Absolutely no one in my friend group had gone further than kissing, and suddenly I was the subject of every piece of graffiti in the bathroom stalls. I ended up breaking up with William a week later because of the teasing I would get in the corridors from people I didn't even know. The entire school knew what I had done at the age of thirteen years old.

Now, I'm not telling this story to say that 'Doing things at thirteen makes you a *slut*! Being a *slut* is *bad*!!' But this was definitely a case of me convincing myself that I was ready, I was in control, and I didn't think about any potential consequences of doing something like that so young. There are a lot of things I'd do differently if I had the chance to start over, even if I do believe in things happening for a reason – for instance, I wouldn't have agreed to marry a guy a week after 'going out' with him. I wouldn't have believed my friends when they told their absurd stories. I wouldn't have given in to peer pressure to start doing sexual things at thirteen. I also wouldn't have lost my virginity at fifteen years old.

Fast forward to 2007. I'm fifteen, and 'going out' with a guy in the year above me who I'd had a crush on for weeks, after shyly asking his friends if he liked me back. He had moved to the UK to study two years prior, had a permanent tan and beautiful blond curly locks, and I was head over heels. Let me set the scene. We'd been 'going out' for three months, we'd been on dates to the cinema every weekend, I'd met his mum, and he'd met my dad (no, my dad didn't like him. My dad hasn't liked any boyfriend I've had. If you pass that test, I'm marrying you). Everything was going great. He was *the one*. It was Good Friday, and I was back at his house after school. His mum was out, and we were on his bed.

'So, do you wanna . . .?' I asked, coming up for air from our make-out session. I'll admit this wasn't the first time I'd asked him if he was ready to go further. I will state here for those who are worried: I wasn't pushy or persistent, and I was also sure he wouldn't agree to anything that made him feel uncomfortable. He'd 'done it' once before, but he seemed really certain that we should wait for the right time. Only this time . . .

'Okay . . . if you're sure you want to.'

I nodded, my heart suddenly pounding and stomach lurching with nerves. *Am I ready? I mean, I can't really back out now*, I thought to myself. *I* do *want to. I'm the one who keeps asking him. I'd look stupid if I changed my mind now.*

If you find yourself in a similar situation, and you have even the slightest shred of doubt in your mind about whether or not you're ready: stop. Do not worry about 'looking stupid', and do not pressure yourself into doing anything you don't want to. It is your body, and your choice.

We got naked, my nerves making me feel sick as I got into position, and then . . .

Ouch. Ow, ow ow ow. It's so much more painful than I thought.

A bit of slow moving, a bit of blood on his sheets, and it was done. I didn't feel like a liberated sexual being. I didn't feel as though I was in heaven. There was absolutely nothing romantic about my 'first time'. Afterwards, my boyfriend seemed more concerned about the blood on his sheets and how he was going to explain it to his mum than about how I felt.

Overall, my 'first time' was painful, unemotional, quick, and although we were safe and used protection, I spent the next couple of weeks panicking that I wouldn't get my next period. If you truly feel ready, then it will not be as horrible as my experience. It may still be a little awkward, and it certainly won't be a perfect experience, but it should not be unbearably painful, and you should feel at ease and reassured by your partner. Do not give in to pressure from your friends, or even from yourself. There is no rush to 'get it out of the way' – I have friends who didn't lose their virginity until far into their twenties. It is not a race. You are ready when you are ready. Oh, and it should go without saying, but just to be crystal clear – make sure you are protected. Safe sex is the only way to avoid unwanted pregnancies and STIs, and if your partner is trying to convince you that 'condoms are gross' or anything similar – get the hell out of there. Don't even look over your shoulder to say goodbye as you walk out of that door.

I actually have a good way to gauge when you are at a stage of being emotionally mature enough to begin to think about doing things of a sexual nature, and that is: if you can sit on the edge of the bed and talk to your partner about STIs, periods and pregnancy, without either of you cringing or getting embarrassed. Also, if you feel as though your partner isn't making you feel completely comfortable about being naked around them, then you are with the wrong partner. Your partner should cherish your body – it should be the most wonderful thing in the world to them. They should make you feel that way, even if you do not feel that way about yourself.

Of course, this isn't a concrete guide – you need to make sure you do not feel pressured and are a hundred per cent comfortable. However, if I'd followed this little rule I made for myself I would have lost my virginity at about twenty-two years old, with the first and only person I've ever been in love with. It would have been special, I would have felt completely ready, and it would've been a much nicer memory to have.

Alas, I suppose it was meant to be this way for me – we live and learn from our mistakes. I hope my story has helped at least one of you reading this to realise that sex – whether it's your first time, or your fiftieth time – should happen when you are ready, emotionally and physically. Don't let anybody try to rush you into something that you know deep down you are not comfortable with. Speaking of which . . .

Assault

I'm sorry, I couldn't sugarcoat the heading. I wouldn't want to lessen the emotional damage that sexual assault can cause. Sexual assault, unfortunately, is tragically common, and can happen in many different ways, but no matter what level of 'severity' someone says you've experienced it at, it can destroy you mentally as much as it can physically, if not more.

Essentially, to put it simply, sexual assault is any instance in which someone is trying to take control of your body in a sexual manner without your permission. That goes for someone slapping your arse in the street, somebody deliberately brushing against you on a packed train, someone you trust refusing to stop when you ask them to and pressuring you into continuing (which is legally considered as rape), or a complete stranger grabbing you and raping you. There are varying legal degrees of 'severity', but at the end of the day, sexual assault is inexcusable, and it is never, ever your fault. It doesn't matter what you're wearing, how far you'd been going with that person, how much you drank – sexual assault is *always* the other party's fault. I myself have experienced sexual assault, to the point where I was terrified for my body, and it's a story I've never told.

It dates back to when I was still living with my dad in my home town. One day I was with him in our local shop. When we got to the checkout, we were served by a boy I found incredibly cute – tall and chiselled (honestly, what more could I ask for?) and only a little older than me, with a great smile. I was twenty years old, and I'd just started making videos on YouTube. This wasn't a case of me being 'young and naive', which is an excuse many use to justify assault. Assault can happen at any age, and at any time, even with people you trust.

I told my dad that I found our cashier cute, and the next time my dad was served by him, bless his heart, he asked for the boy's number for me! We started texting, and arranged to go on a date. Our 'first date' went pretty well, although I realised very early on that he was very hands-on. We went to a laser tag place in our town, before getting coffee. Every time he found me in the laser tag game, instead of shooting at me, he would pull me close to him, making out with me. I already knew in my mind that, as much as I fancied him, his level of affection was weirding me out – but not wanting to be 'rude' (facepalm) I went along with it.

After our coffee (he left me alone to drink his latte, thankfully) we walked to the bus station so he could catch his bus, all with him wrapping his arms around me and making out. At this point, I was completely confused. I knew I *liked* him, but as I'd got older, that level of PDA made me feel uncomfortable. Looking back, it was obvious I should have told him to get lost, that he was making me feel weird, and walked away. However, even at twenty, I was scared of being seen as 'frigid' (which is a horrible fucking word, by the way), and I was also scared of him getting angry. I should have let this 'first date' be the end of it – but when he texted me that night asking if I wanted to hang out at his house at the week-end, I said yes.

I have to state this here: if you ever feel anything like I did, do NOT agree to meet at that person's house, especially if you don't know them all that well and they're too 'heavy' for you. There is so much that I regret about the situation I'm describing.

That Saturday morning, before leaving for this guy's house, I had a panic attack. A full-blown panic attack, on my bedroom floor, my entire body pleading with me not to go to his house. But I'd *promised* him, right? I couldn't back out now (yes, Emma, you could have, and *should* have). Once I calmed down, I went downstairs and told my dad how I felt. Seeing the obvious unease on my face, he told me in no uncertain terms that I shouldn't go – but

I was adamant, and I persisted, much to his dismay. Reluctantly, he told me to take his car and drive there instead of getting the bus, so that I could leave on my own terms. He also instructed me to text him a certain word if I felt unsafe and needed a phone call to get me out of there.

My dad is the best human on the entire fucking planet.

Twenty minutes later (yes, I drove after a panic attack – also don't do that, for crying out loud) I was outside the guy's house. He came out to meet me, and led me inside. He offered me a drink and showed me around. His parents were out, and it was just the two of us. Finally, he led me into his bedroom – and that's when it started.

He took the glass of juice out of my hand and began to grab me by the waist, kissing me roughly. This time, I began to pull away – I couldn't handle my lack of control in this situation. In response, he laughed.

'What's up?' he asked, before grabbing me by the waist again, this time picking me up and lifting me off the floor. If you know anything about me, you know that I am very short, and very light – there was zero way I could wrestle my way out of his grasp as he carried me over to his bed. He pressed me down on to his bed underneath him, kissing me again. His legs were either side of my body, his breath on my neck as he began to grope my chest. I began to feel sick. I was *trapped*. My heart began to pound as my mind raced over the possibilities: should I just go along with it, so that he didn't get angry? Should I try and run?

Fortunately, fight-or-flight mode began to kick in. As soon as his lips left mine for a split second, I pushed him to the side as though I was about to straddle him, and rolled off the bed, quickly standing up and grabbing my phone and texting my dad the word he'd told me to send him. The boy simply sat there on his bed, bemused. I should have grabbed my keys and run, but I was afraid of him taking off after me, then me getting lost in his house and him catching up with me, incensed. Adrenalin was coursing through me as I weighed up my options, as the boy stared at me, frowning. Just then, my phone rang.

'Hello?'

'Hi, honey, I'm afraid you'll have to come home, your boss just rang. He's trying to get hold of you but a delivery's come in and he needs an extra pair of hands.'

'Oh, are you sure? Fine, okay. I'll leave now.'

Hanging up, relieved, I grabbed my keys.

'I'm sorry,' I said, trying my best to look truthful (I'm a horrible liar because I never do it!). 'My boss needs my help, I have to rush into work.'

'They can't do that,' the boy replied, standing up. 'And besides, why would he call your dad?'

'He couldn't get through to me,' I said quickly, walking downstairs. The boy was following close behind me. 'My phone keeps screwing up. I'll text you later.'

And with that, I opened his front door, walked towards my dad's car and quickly got in, locking it and driving away as the boy stood at his front door, seemingly bewildered. I sped home, feeling complete relief to be out of that situation. If I hadn't arranged with my dad to text him a code word in an emergency, how far would this guy have gone? To this day, I don't know what would have happened, and I'm just so glad that I got out safely.

As soon as I got home, I checked Facebook, and saw that the guy had posted a status consisting of one simple word, 'Ugh'. I quickly unfriended him, blocked his number, and never contacted him again. I saw him a couple of times in the shop, but ducked away before he could see me. There is so much that I would do differently now. I would have pushed him away in the laser tag on our first date. I wouldn't have arranged to see him again. I certainly wouldn't have gone to his house knowing we were likely to be alone, especially as I barely knew him.

However, I'm also a lot more headstrong than I was back then – I know that none of what happened was my fault. It wasn't my fault that I felt scared of being seen as 'frigid' – that was on *him* for making me feel that way. It wasn't my fault that he 'expected' something to happen when I went to his house – that was *his* assumption, and his alone. I also know that there will be some people reading this and thinking, *Well, you went there alone, what did you expect?* To which I say: you're a part of the problem. I'm not the scared little girl that I was back then: take responsibility for how you make others feel when it comes to getting physical with them.

This wasn't fun to write – this was a memory I have definitely tried to repress over the years. Please take something from this story: you always, *always* have the right to say no. You have a right to feel safe in someone's presence, not scared. If someone thinks you're 'frigid' for not wanting to 'do stuff' with them, let them think it. *Own* it. Be 'frigid' and proud. Only you get to decide what happens to your body – no matter who else in your life thinks otherwise.

Also, shop boy, with the nice cheekbones and the unsexiest

level of respect a man could have, I don't know how else to say this. I want to wish you the best, and hope that the years have matured you. I have considered my words carefully, and contemplated being mature and only printing words that will reflect my feelings about you in years to come – so, honestly and sincerely, with as much love as I can muster, from me to you: I don't wish for karma to strike down hard on you. I'm cutting out the part where I say 'I wish you develop erectile dysfunction'. I simply hope that you no longer treat women the way you treated me – like an object. Like an opportunity to 'get some'. Equally, I also hope that no one ever makes you feel pressured and uncomfortable the way that you did with me – you may not know this, but it is a horrible scenario to put anyone in. I hope you have seen the error of your ways.

For anyone who finds themself in a similar situation to the one I was in, I have some tips:

> Have an emergency contact. Having my dad call me was the reason I was able to escape the situation I was in. I simply do not know how much more dangerous it would have gotten without an escape clause. Quite simply, if you are considering going to meet someone and you do not feel one hundred per cent comfortable: do not go. However, if you feel at ease, and then something about the situation changes, send a

discreet text to a close friend or family member asking them to call you.

↯ Do not be afraid of the word 'no'. Of course, each situation is unique, and I do not know the temperament of the person making you feel uneasy, but more often than not, if you loudly state that you are uncomfortable and wish for someone to stop, then they will. As frustrating as it is, some people may simply not realise they are upsetting you unless you make your feelings vocal. Of course, in rare cases, others *will* know what they are doing to you, and continue – it is equally important to vocally state that you are uncomfortable. What you must not do is stay quiet and 'go along' with something that makes you feel uncomfortable. If your gut feeling is to leave, then do.

↯ Always tell someone about what has happened, regardless of how far it went – if you felt uneasy at any point, then it is *not* your fault. You are not 'frigid', you are not 'lame' or 'uncool' or any other word that that person may have used to try and get you to continue. If you revoked consent at any point and that person did not immediately stop, then it is sexual assault. Talk about what happened with an adult that can help advise you on what further steps you should take. There are also helplines at the back of this book with professionals who are advised on the laws surrounding your situation and equipped with knowledge on what to do. Remember: it was not your fault, you are not being 'silly', and you are not alone.

Coming Out

For the longest time, I have avoided the requests to talk about 'coming out'. I never felt qualified (and to an extent, I still don't) to talk about something I didn't really experience, and it wasn't until recently, when I made a video finally talking about my sexuality, that I realised I'd been struggling internally with accepting who I am and telling those closest to me.

Now, let me be clear – I am not saying that I am a lesbian or bisexual. The truth is, even in my mid-twenties, I still don't really know. In 2016, I made a video called 'I am sexually confused' where I spoke openly about my confusion for the first time – despite spending the entire night dreading a phone call from my parents after it was uploaded. (That's not to say they're homophobic people – you just don't know how others will react to the idea of you being attracted to people of the same sex in any way.) I finally felt comfortable enough with myself at the age of twenty-four to put my fears of judgement aside to try and help others who were going through the same, who might see the video and not feel so alone. As I sat there, looking at my phone, anxious at the thought of my parents texting me to tell me they were 'disappointed' or something – or worse, not talking to me at all – I realised that I have had this same internalised fear since I was about fourteen years old.

There was a girl in my school who ended up in all of my classes – and to me, she was perfect. She was beautiful, confident, funny . . . everyone liked her. No, everyone *worshipped* her. Even the bullies that picked on me daily left her completely alone. To me, she was the coolest girl I knew, and for the next two years, I didn't know whether I wanted to be her or be with her. I began to hang around with her friend group at lunchtimes (although they often did their best to avoid me – more about this later) and I quickly changed everything about me in order to seem 'cool' to her. I listened to the bands she loved, I copied her fashion sense and hair colour. I was jealous of every friend she was closer to – and all I wanted to do was to be able to kiss her.

The thing is – and this is what was so confusing, being a teenager with no guidebooks on this sort of thing – that was as far as I could imagine going sexually with her. I could imagine holding her hand and kissing her, but the thought of doing further things of a sexual nature with her made me feel uncomfortable. Confused, I began to tell my friends that I was bisexual (this wasn't something I was necessarily scared of doing – back in 2007, in the days of MySpace, it was *cool* to be emo and bisexual. Well, at least to other bisexual emos, it was). I was convinced that I was able to have crushes on guys and girls – but it was like having a crush without a sexual urge. I began getting drunk at my local skate park and making out with other drunk girls, trying to work out who I was. When you are younger, there is so much pressure to put a label on yourself, as everyone around you wants to put you in a certain box – gay, straight, bi, goth, nerd – and I decided for myself that I fitted into the 'bi' box. I definitely cared about the girl in my year, more than 'just a friend' would – but I just couldn't imagine doing more than kissing her.

Not that it mattered – she was straight. After a little while, word about my 'crush' on this girl got around, and one day in biology class, whilst I was sitting at the workbench with her and her friends, she turned to me and said, 'Well, we all know you've got a crush on me. Would you make out with me?'

Blushing as her friends looked at me, giggling, I shook my head and stared fiercely into my science book, wishing for the ground to swallow me up.

'No.'

'Oh, don't lie, yes you would,' one of her friends said, and they all laughed again. Much to my relief, our biology teacher must have been listening to the conversation and told us all off for talking, and that was that. Being humiliated for having feelings for my friend and being 'called out' for them in front of the people I desperately wanted to like me was one of the worst experiences I had during my school life. Shortly after that, my feelings for her began to fade.

I later found out from the comments on my video about being confused that what I'd experienced was a 'squish' – a crush but without any sexual desire. A longing to be in a romantic relationship with someone without necessarily wanting to have sex with them. Since that video, I have found a 'label' that I can always apply to myself if I ever feel the need (which I don't): I am bi-romantic. I can fall in love with males and females, but I'm not sure if I could ever be sexually attracted to a female. Perhaps one day I'll find myself in the right situation, where I feel comfortable and want to explore that side of my sexuality. Perhaps I *am* bisexual. Perhaps social conditioning has suppressed how I feel about girls, especially seeing as I'm far more into ladies when I'm drunk. If you're told by society when you're growing up that being gay is a *bad thing*, your brain will do what it needs for you to feel accepted by others – and that can include quashing your desires and feeling ashamed for being different.

However, the feeling of dread I had as a teenager at the thought of my parents finding out I was *bisexual* was a horrible experience. I'd convinced myself that that's what I was, and I was fine telling my friends about it – but the fear of my mum and dad finding out and kicking me out of the house for it ran through my mind constantly throughout my teenage years. I am by nature a very anxious person. I struggle with *catastrophic thinking* – automatically imagining the worst scenario for every decision I make in my life. I hid my 'orientation' option on MySpace, just in case my dad discovered what MySpace actually *was* and somehow found my profile. Any time I selected 'prefer not to say' on a form, I was paranoid that my answer would somehow get back to my parents. I hid how I felt about people of the same sex right up until I acknowledged my feelings in that video in 2016 – and even then at the age of twenty-four, I sat by my phone for hours, dreading that I was no longer somebody's daughter.

There is a happy ending to my story. No longer able to take the silence, I called my dad, and to my surprise, he answered. I asked if he'd seen my latest video, and even then tried to play it off: 'Oh, you know, it's just YouTube,' despite meaning every word I'd said. My dad simply laughed, jokingly teasing me (this sounds mean, but I promise you he was trying to make me feel at ease), and that was it. We changed the subject. Everything was fine. Hanging up, I felt a rush of confidence like I'd never had before – I *was* fine the way I was, being able to love men and women. I was also, in a strange way, angry. I had been hiding who I was from the people who cared about me the most for absolutely no reason other than my own internal fears. Since then, I have been a lot more open about how I feel – being able to fall in love with twice as many people is no longer a weakness to me, but a strength. Perhaps one day, I'll meet the right woman, and fall in love, and be just as happy as I could potentially be with a man. However, I believe that sexuality is fluid. Your sexuality could change the second you meet the right person, with the right set of traits and chromosomes that will seem almost tailor-made just for you. As you get older, you definitely become more confident with who you are as a person – I am living proof – although my happy ending is not always shared by others struggling with their own identity.

Living at home and feeling terrified to tell your parents or other loved ones about your sexuality can be a horrible thing to go through. I completely ruled out having a girlfriend for the entire time I lived at home, just in case my parents found out and happened to get mad (I know now that they probably would have been fine with it after the initial shock). I felt 'lucky' to still be attracted to people of the opposite sex so that I could avoid the question entirely – but this isn't the case for those who identify as gay or lesbian. I cannot imagine hearing questions from family members such as, 'So, when are you going to get a boyfriend/girlfriend?' when you cannot think of anything less desirable. This also applies to those who identify as asexual – feeling 'wrong' for not being sexually attracted to anyone, male or female or other, and being told that you 'Just haven't found the right person yet'!

I didn't address my sexuality with my family until I was twenty-four years old. I wasn't living at home and was completely independent from their income. In my mind, I had played out so many worst-case scenarios: being removed from the family, kicked out with nowhere to go – I know now that none of this would have happened, but because of my fear, I suppressed the person that I truly was until I was able to survive on my own just in case. Because I was far too scared of the reaction I would receive, I never 'came out' in the traditional way of sitting my parents down and telling them. I kept telling myself, *If I just date boys, I won't have to come out at all*, so I cannot say that I have been in the same situation as so many of you, struggling to talk about your identity.

There are some helplines given at the back of this book that will allow you to talk to a professional who will be able to advise you about how to come out. However, my one piece of advice I would definitely give to anyone struggling is to find another family member – perhaps an aunt or an older cousin – who would be willing to accompany you and support you when you tell your parents. Coming out can be a shock to others, and lead to them immediately acting irrationally. Having another calm adult in the same room can help your parents/loved ones see that you are still the same person they have always known and loved. If you are coming out after getting into a relationship with someone of the same sex, and their own parents know and are accepting of their sexuality, ask for them to be present when you tell your family. I cannot guarantee your family will accept you – I do not know them. However, I do know that you are wonderful as you are, and your sexual orientation does not define how kind you are, or how intelligent and funny you are, and it certainly doesn't turn you into a monster as soon as others find out. Your heart will continue beating after you come out as gay/bi/pan/ace/other – and we are slowly but surely becoming a world where the younger, more accepting generation are becoming the older generation. Homophobia and prejudice will sadly always exist in some form across the world, but in our lifetime, we will be one step closer to fewer teen suicides linked to sexuality. This has given me comfort many times over the years. If I have children in the future, they will have nothing to fear if they discover that they are on the LGBTQ+ spectrum. We are the more accepting future.

7

Bad Friends

How To Spot A Bad Friend

Let me make something perfectly clear: you're going to have a bad friend in your lifetime. It doesn't matter if you're a Regular Joe or Taylor Swift. There is going to be at least one person in your life who will try to take advantage of you or make you feel small, all under the disguise of being a 'friend'. I myself have had so many of what I would now consider 'bad friends' (and been hurt/let down/ betrayed so many times) that I learned quite early on to love my own company – which isn't a bad thing, by the way! Always remain your own best friend. You have to put up with yourself for eighty years!

Before we go on to listing my own criteria to assess if someone may be a 'bad friend', please etch this into your brain – you have a right to remove bad people from your life. You have a right not to be disrespected by someone you trust. Of course, someone letting you down for a movie date one time doesn't make them a 'bad friend' – but repeated actions that make you suspect that someone you care about doesn't care about you all that much should be enough to tell you to get outta that friendship!

If you're starting to wonder if your friend is worth keeping around, here are some telltale red flags of a 'bad friend':

- Does this person often let you down at the last minute? Do they agree to hang out with you at the weekend and then always seem to cancel with just a couple of hours to spare? Cancelling once or twice isn't cause to drop that person – shit happens – but if this is the sixth time their grandmother has died, the chances are they want to spend their time doing something else. Their loss.

- Does your friend often make jokes at your expense, even when they know you're not laughing along? If this person is nice to you when you're alone with them, but then joins in with jokes about you in front of others, especially if you've already told them how much it upsets you, the chances are they don't really care about your feelings. Explain to them how these jokes make you feel, and if they say something along the lines of, 'Oh, lighten up!' or, 'It's just a joke!' instead of apologising, that's a bad sign.

❧ Does this person talk about you behind your back? This is an obvious one. If you keep finding out from other people that your 'friend' is bitching about you when you're not around, or joins in when others are bitching about you rather than defending you, they're not being a good friend. Period.

❧ Does this person spill your secrets? Listen, secrets aren't easy to keep, especially if you're at school – sadly, gossiping and having the 'scoop' on someone can make you more liked in the short-term by others that dislike the person you're gossiping about. If your friend tells someone a huge secret you've only entrusted to them, then that person isn't looking out for your well-being.

❧ Does your friend make excuses not to see you? This is different to cancelling on you at the last minute, this is them ducking you altogether. Some people are shy, and simply don't want to hang out with others outside where they have to, such as at school or work, but if this person is often out with others, or hanging out with a big group of people at school and they make an effort to avoid you or continually decline to hang out, they don't value their time with you. Try to find someone who sees hanging out with you as something that matters to them.

As I mentioned in the last chapter, there was a girl in my school year I had a 'crush' (actually a 'squish') on between the ages of fourteen and sixteen. Because she had such a bold, positive outlook, and because she was kind and funny, she was extremely popular with the indie/emo kids that I considered 'cool'. In fact, there was a whole group of people that she would hang around with every break and lunchtime – and it was a clique I was desperate to be a part of. This group of about ten kids had all known each other for years – they always hung out together inside and outside school, every weekend without fail, and were basically known to the *real* popular kids as the 'weird emos'. That didn't matter to me – they were squad *goals*. As someone who was ... admittedly a bit ... well, *weird* at school, I usually hung out either by myself, or with the one friend I'd managed to make (when she wasn't hanging out with girls that she had more in common with). It became my dream to be accepted into the 'weird emos' – and every lunchtime I would make a beeline for them, with the theory, *If I keep hanging out with them, eventually they'll just accept me into their clique.*

For the first couple of weeks, this pretty much worked. I would find them out on the school field, sit with them, laugh at their jokes, pretend to like the same indie bands as them – but over time, I started to notice little changes that made me feel unwelcome in their clique. I would see photos posted on MySpace of them all hanging out at the weekend (I wasn't invited), I would be ignored in conversation, and after a few weeks, they stopped hanging out in their usual spot on the school field. By the time I found them, either in a music room, or in a classroom, it would be the end of lunch. Looking back, it was obvious to me that they would all arrange to meet up somewhere without telling me (I only had a few of their phone numbers, and none would ever text me back) so that I wouldn't be able to find them. At the time, I tried denying it to myself: *Perhaps the field was just too cold. They're not doing it on purpose*, but that didn't stop me feeling completely rejected, which just made me seek out their approval more. Now, I wish to state here that I am not saying people you like *have* to hang around with you – they have as much right to feel comfortable around you as you do around others – but if people that you consider your 'friends' are doing this to you, then they do not want to be around you. It sounds tough, but you have to get the hint. Move on, walk away, and stop trying to change who you are to make others like you. If I'd heard that as an insecure, rejected fifteen-year-old, and if I'd actually listened to the advice, I would have spent way less time feeling hurt and trying to fit in, and more time focusing on studying and making time for people who would have appreciated my company.

Okay, so what about when someone you consider a 'friend' upsets you, but then apologises? I mean, I just told you that friends who do you wrong aren't worth keeping around, right? How many times can someone do you wrong before you decide to cut them off? Well, for this, I would simply say trust your instincts. You will know your 'friend' better than I do – you will know when they seem genuinely remorseful for something they've done wrong. Don't accept a half-hearted apology. If you think someone is apologising simply because they feel as though they *have* to, or even worse, because a group project is coming up and you're the one that's doing all the work . . . trust yourself. Don't relent and accept an apology that will only enable you to be hurt again in the future.

However – I always believe in second chances. Give someone the benefit of the doubt at least one time. Sometimes, people make genuine mistakes. They may not be good at owning up to their faults and may find it hard to apologise. I myself am pretty stubborn. I will admit that in the past I have often fought to defend my intentions even though I knew deep down I was in the wrong (more about that later). If your friend has only let you down once, forgive them. Trust them. However, if they continue to repeat their mistakes without learning from them, and you continue to feel let down, hurt or disrespected, keep your head high and walk away. It's definitely hard to do, but in the long run, you will be happier. There's a famous saying: 'Fool me once, shame on you. Fool me twice, shame on me.'

As for me? I went through a stage where I felt as though I didn't have anyone – I'd grown apart from my school friends, and I found it hard to trust anyone in the YouTube community in an act of self-preservation. I was convinced that all my peers hated me, and I became extremely reserved. I've never hated my own company – in fact, I love being alone. However, as I've got older, and past indiscretions have been forgotten, I have made an effort to seek out friends who care about me and enjoy hanging out with me. I have people in my life now who share my love of things such as wrestling or films, with whom I share many inside jokes, and who genuinely look forward to seeing me, without shutting me down or making excuses. These are people who don't let me down, who don't use me and who care about my well-being.

Ten years ago, my life was filled with people who did the

opposite. If I can go from being the loner who was ditched at every given opportunity to finding happiness in friendship, I promise that there is hope for you. The right people will come along, and when they do, hold on to them, and go the extra mile to treat them with love and respect. When you make a mistake, own up to it and apologise. Engage in open and honest communication. Good friendships are like flowers (gross, Emma, how cheesy): water them, and they'll last. Fake flowers may seem nice from a distance, but when you stare at them in detail, you realise they're not real, and no matter how much you water them they're still fake. What even is this analogy?

When You're The Bad Friend

Okay, so we've spoken a lot about 'bad friends' – the people you should walk away from when they wrong you purposefully and repeatedly – but what happens when that 'bad friend' . . . is you?

Over the course of your life, you're going to screw up. You're going to get carried away with a joke, or fail to defend someone for fear of looking stupid. You're going to take something the wrong way and lash out, or be too stubborn to end an argument and apologise, even if you know you're in the wrong. I've done all these things over the course of my lifetime, and I'm someone who would consider herself extremely loyal to friends.

I have been the 'bad friend'.

If you happened to stumble across my YouTube channel between 2013 and 2014, you would have been aware that I wasn't often seen without a girl called Cherry sewn to my hip. I'll go on record here and tell you all that Cherry is one of the loveliest, kindest people

I've ever had the pleasure of knowing. I'm hoping that she won't mind me telling you all this story, as – I will admit – I was completely in the wrong when we fell out during the summer of 2014.

Cherry and I had first met at a YouTube party back in late 2012, right after I sat down at a make-up table and grabbed a bottle of foundation to look at, only for her to march on over and tell me in no uncertain terms, 'Excuse me, that's mine.' I knew from that moment on that we were destined to be the baddest bitches in the community, and from then on, we were joined at the hip. I visited her often, we made videos together at her house and even co-owned our own beauty/fashion collaboration channel. Of course, we sometimes did things that the other person didn't agree with, but we were, for the most part, inseparable. I thought our friendship was tighter than anyone else's. I didn't realise that I was unwittingly treating her badly as a friend.

Fast forward to late summer 2014. The YouTube community, fans and creators alike, were getting prepared for Summer in the City, a YouTube convention held in London every August. A couple of weeks before the event, Cherry and I got into an argument over some things that I had said a while back, not knowing that they had upset her. Instead of acting rationally, as I would now, three years on – instead of putting my friendship with her above my own pride and *apologising* for how I had made her feel – I got defensive. I refused to believe I had done anything wrong. I wasn't a *bad friend*! Without leaving myself even a second to cool off, I completely passed the blame back to her, and just like that, our very public close friendship was over. Over the next few weeks, we unfollowed and unfriended each other on every social media website and we were no longer on speaking terms.

For an entire year after our argument, Cherry and I didn't say a word to one another. It wasn't until Summer in the City the next year that I saw her in the green room. We exchanged glances. In the twelve months that had passed since we'd fallen out, my anger had completely died away, now replaced by regret and sorrow for the loss of someone I'd been so close to. In front of me wasn't the person who had hurt me, but the person that *I* had hurt, and who I had been too stubborn to apologise to. Taking a deep breath and finally swallowing my pride, I walked towards her, expecting her to walk away. She would have had every right to – but she didn't. We went outside, shared an awkward exchange, and hugged. We both talked over how we'd handled the situation (and let me be clear, I definitely handled it worse than she did), and she graciously accepted my apology. When the time came, we walked away from each other, knowing the air was a little clearer.

I am grateful that this story has a happy ending. Over the past three years since our argument, I have made it my mission to become a better person each and every day, and I am happy to say that I am a great distance from the stubborn, proud fool that I was in 2014. Cherry and I are close again, albeit not as close as we were before, and I have done everything I can to show her how much I regret how I handled our argument, which would have been resolved had I not been so quick to anger at having my ego dented. The only real positive, along with learning my lesson, is that our friendship is definitely more equal and honest than it was when we were inseparable. It has taken an awfully long time for Cherry to feel as though she can treat me like a friend again – with good reason. I have paid for my sins by enduring three years of the loss of a truly great friendship, ruined by the rift I helped cause. Sometimes, you can be so blinded by the rage that you convince yourself is justified that you cannot see the hurt that you are causing – and once that rage has subsided, you are left with nothing but a room filled with regrets.

Cherry and I talk most days now, although I would completely accept it if she never spoke to me again. She didn't have to forgive me, but she chose to, despite all that I had done to escalate our relationship breakdown. I cannot say I would have been able to be as gracious as she was if I was in her position.

If you feel as though your ego has been dented, and you feel enraged, it can be easy to fire back heated words out of anger and say things you don't mean, which can ruin a friendship for ever. If I had taken a day – or even a few hours – and responded to Cherry after I had calmed down, who knows where we'd be right now? The chances are, if I'd calmly apologised, taken responsibility for my part in our argument, we'd still be as close as we were before, possibly even closer. Instead, I chose the quick, easy thing to do and acted defensively, forever tainting our relationship. Sometimes, you will be the 'bad friend'. Sometimes, you have to bite the bullet and apologise, and do what you need to do to make it up to that friend. Communication is the foundation of a good relationship – it is so important to communicate your feelings calmly, as well as being able to put your pride aside and listen to what your friend or partner is saying, because they are not expressing their feelings for nothing. You must be as willing to listen as you are willing to defend yourself. If you feel the need to defend your actions, make sure that you are not simply defending them out of hurt and anger. Explain your side of the story, calmly and with respect – it may just save a relationship from breaking down.

This entire situation has changed me a lot – I am no longer afraid to put my pride aside and apologise when I am wrong. I no longer try to pass the blame off on others, and now wait until I'm calm before responding. There is no shame in saying to someone, 'I need a moment to process this, I'll speak to you about it in a while,' if you need to gather your thoughts. I don't plan on making the same mistakes ever again with any friends in the future. It's just a shame that I had to lose my friendship with Cherry temporarily in order to learn how to treat other friends with the respect I should have always shown.

And, Cherry, in case you need to hear it again, despite me boring you with the same words over and over again, I'm so, so sorry. You're still my caramel crème.

Peer Pressure

Everyone, at some point in their lives, will experience peer pressure. Whether it's a colleague begging you to go to the office party, friends chanting 'Chug! Chug! Chug!' at the pub, or friends handing you a marker and telling you that writing graffiti on the school wall isn't a 'big deal', we'll all experience a battle between our morals and our desire to be seen as 'cool'. As I have said, at a young age I was insecure, and therefore very impressionable. I thought I was 'uncool', and that by doing the things that the 'cool' kids were doing, I would be 'cool' too. After feeling rejected by the 'weird emos' that I so wanted to accept me, I went in search of a new group of people to hang around with (yes, I was *that* uncomfortable with being alone, fearing that being on my own would attract attention from the bullies) and found company in a smaller group of girls in the year above.

No matter which year you're in at school, anybody in the year above you is cooler than you. It's a natural hierarchy. They seem more mature, as though they have their lives in order. They're smarter, funnier, and if you're able to get in with them, then kids in your own year will see you as cool, right? That's what went through my head when I was fifteen years old and first hanging around with a girl we'll call 'Kat'. Kat was the cool friend you read about in young adult novels – sixteen years old, with tattoos that she got by pretending she was older, openly lesbian and yet left completely alone by the bullies that would pick on anyone else for being the same, and seemingly the most confident girl I knew. For lack of a better word, to me, she was *awesome*, and everything I wanted to be. I didn't have to pretend I was someone else around her, and she and her cool friends were seemingly fine with me hanging around with them at lunchtime after I found myself ditched by the 'weird emos' clique in my own school year. I'm still unsure on how I felt about Kat, but looking back, I remember imagining kissing her and doing *other stuff* without feeling like I was forcing the idea on myself. To me, Kat was the coolest, most incredibly perfect girl I knew.

One slight catch, though – she was a smoker.

Now, I'm not about to shame you if you're a smoker – the beauty of living on this planet is our freedom of choice – however, at fifteen, the idea of smoking totally grossed me out. I'd seen my dad smoke throughout my childhood, having a cigarette as soon as he woke up, before and after every meal, and I'd also watched him give up cold turkey after a stint in hospital, coughing his guts up as his lungs began to recover. I swore to myself and to my father that I would never smoke. I swore I would never get addicted and go through the health problems that my dad had experienced – and I also took comfort in knowing that if I was ever caught smoking, I would be in more than serious trouble with both of my parents.

But Kat was *cool*. And *gorgeous*.

When she first offered me a puff of her cigarette on the school field, us both sitting in a circle with about five or six of her other friends, I stuttered a quiet 'N-no, thanks' before looking down, *ashamed* of myself! *Ashamed* for standing by my morals! I felt my cheeks blush bright red as she shrugged, passing her cigarette to another one of her friends. I'd just shown her and all her pals how uncool I was – how I was still just a dorky fifteen-year-old who couldn't hang with the cool kids. I vowed from that moment on that any time Kat offered me an opportunity to be on her level, I would take it. I wanted her to like me. I wanted all her friends to like me.

The next time Kat offered me her cigarette, I took it.

I can vividly remember doing it wrong and spluttering and coughing, my lungs feeling as though they were on fire. I probably looked less cool trying to smoke than I did when I'd refused to smoke in the first place. However, I persevered. In a vain attempt to match Kat in *effortless cool*, I gave up my morals, going against everything I'd stood for, and began smoking with my new gang at lunchtimes. I have bittersweet memories of walking to the back of the school field, where no teacher could be bothered to walk, to light up with Kat and her friends, popping a breath mint in my mouth and spraying myself with cheap perfume before our next class started. Within a few days, word had got around in my own year that I was smoking, and most of the kids (including all of the 'weird emos') thought I was an idiot. I no longer cared. I had the approval of Kat and her friends, and they didn't judge me. Soon enough, the one cigarette shared between friends at lunchtime turned into one cigarette of my own that I myself would pass around the circle, which then turned into me smoking by myself before and after school.

Without even realising it, I'd become addicted to cigarettes, and I was no longer doing it to be cool. I'd go into the corner shop by our school before classes began, heart racing as I tried to fool the staff there that I was old enough to buy cigarettes. I would stuff the pack of cigarettes (the cheapest you could buy) deep into the bottom of my bag, sometimes taking them out of their box and keeping them stashed away in the zip-up inside pocket, in case my dad went down my school bag at home. I was losing what few friends I had in my year, lying to my teachers and parents, and had gone against everything I'd believed about cigarettes in order to look 'cool'.

Eventually, I realised that most of my pocket money – which my dad trusted me to spend on sweets and nice things – was being drained by my smoking habit, and it was only then that I truly realised what I was doing. If my dad knew what I'd been doing with his money, spending it on something that had plagued him for over forty years of his life, he wouldn't be so much angry as disappointed. From then on, I stopped buying cigarettes (I don't remember it being too difficult to kick the habit – I was only on about five a day at my worst, but that was more than enough to waste most of my money and make me think about my next

cigarette opportunity all day during class) and I distanced myself
from Kat and her friends, choosing to spend the rest of the year
with a couple of acquaintances in the school library. It was
extremely difficult to stop hanging around with my 'friends',
avoiding any scenario where I'd have to explain why. I missed
them, awfully. I was no longer 'in' with them, by choice, and
wasn't 'in' with anyone in my own year. Eventually, the end of
the school year rolled around, and Kat and her friends left. I never
saw them again. Sometimes I check up on Kat on Facebook, just
to see how she's doing. She seems happy.

I never told my parents about any of this, so if they're still reading, I'm sorry. Just know that I learned a lot about myself during
that short time, and imagining the disappointment I would have
faced from you both was enough to make me realise that I didn't
need to do something stupid to become 'more' of a person – and
neither does anyone reading this. If someone that you care about
tries to make you do something you don't want to do, don't fear
looking 'uncool' or 'stupid'. Kat shouldn't have continued to offer
me cigarettes after I originally said no, but I also shouldn't have
gone against everything I stood for in order to impress someone.
If someone is really your friend, they won't try to pressure you
into anything, and they won't judge you for not doing something
like smoking cigarettes. Looking back, I realise that Kat and her
friends weren't even too bothered by me not taking up Kat's offer
of a cigarette the first time – most of that shame I felt that made
me want to try again was from myself. I had convinced myself,
in part due to my lack of self-esteem, that I'd made Kat and her
friends think as low of me as I thought of myself. Peer pressure
is also what led me to want to start being sexually active at such

a young age, in an attempt to 'keep up' with others. If you are thinking of doing something that you do not want to do purely to change how someone thinks of you – remember this: at some point in your life, you are going to be the only person you've got. You'll only be answering to yourself – and when that time comes, will your decisions have been worth it? Will you be proud of the choices you made?

8

Education

(and making the most of it)

Embracing The Inner Nerd

I feel as though we've spoken a lot about school already, but seeing as it was quite frankly one of the worst periods of my life, and knowing that a lot of you reading this right now are currently still going through it, I definitely think it deserves its own chapter. I don't know what school is like for you – whether you enjoy it, if you're home-schooled, or if your school wherever you are in the world just isn't that bad – but I had an awful experience. I dealt with bullies, bitching and gossiping, bad friends, as well as some teachers who didn't seem to care about what they were teaching. All of that on top of having the pressure of, 'IF YOU FAIL THIS EXAM YOU WON'T GET A JOB AND YOU'LL END UP HOMELESS.' It's safe to say my time in secondary school wasn't great.

At school, all I really cared about was getting cool kids to like me. I was obsessed with getting a hold of the latest bag or backpack, finding out who was going out with who, or working out how to break the rules to look cool without actually getting into trouble. Like I've already made clear – I wasn't a popular kid. I had thick, jet-black hair, two dark rings of eyeliner big enough to make me look like a drugged-up panda, and was dressed in the cheapest shirts and trousers my family could get. When I outgrew my school blazer, my mum cut off the patch and sewed it on to a cheap non-official blazer that was miles too big for me, and I was teased for it for the next four years (yes, I stopped growing at twelve. I was actually one of the tallest kids in my school when I was ten).

My point is that hardly any of my time went towards my education – I would skip most of my homework, doing the bare minimum necessary to avoid detention, leaving any coursework until the night before and trying to cram nine months of revision into the one hour before my final exam. I will state here that as a teenager, I was a mixture of smart and lucky (is 'smucky' a word? It is now). I did pretty well in my exams, all things considered. You know that one kid in your class that would act like a smart-arse and do hardly any schoolwork, but was still somehow top of the class? That was me. I'm sorry. I suppose that in my arrogant mind, I thought I didn't *need* to revise, as I knew I'd at least pass all of my classes – but that meant that, instead of studying, my mind was on other things which, looking back, were a complete waste of my time.

Here's some advice you might not like, and you might not heed it: do your homework the night you get it. Make time to revise for at least three hours a night in the weeks leading up to your exams. Take as many notes as you need to and always ask your teachers for help with anything you don't understand. I know that most of you won't listen to this advice, because I didn't listen to it when I was given it, either. Only, I'm not going to shame you for not listening. How can I tell you what to do if I didn't do it myself? It's definitely advice that I *wish* I'd listened to, but when you're at school, education is usually the last thing on your mind.

There was one time when my cockiness didn't pay off, however. During our final two school years of ICT (computing for those without stupid abbreviations) we ended up with a new teacher that no one had ever had before. She was intimidating, adorned with bizarre jewellery and nails longer than diving boards. Over the next two years, we all began to suspect her heart wasn't in it. Our coursework was a mishmash of databases and reports, and without the right guidance, none of us really had much of a clue what to actually do. We'd walk into her classroom and see her flicking through paperwork, frowning uncertainly before getting us to take our seats at the computers. Because she didn't seem to care, we didn't care either – surely so long as we did as we were told, we'd pass, right? Our coursework would take us about ten minutes per lesson, and then the rest of the hour was ours. Quickly, ICT became everyone's favourite lesson – do a bit of database work, and then sit and play games or check our MySpaces. (I realise I mention MySpace a lot, but this was 2007, and my MySpace profile was my entire life, thank you very much.)

One day towards the end of our final school year, our teacher sat us down, stony-faced. She told us that she had misunderstood our course, and that none of our coursework was what it was supposed to be. Some of us managed to scrape an E, the minimum grade, but most of us had completely failed. Suddenly, we weren't the lazy, cocky students we'd been for two years – now, we were all bolt-upright, horrified at the thought of our coursework dragging down our final grade. Even though I managed to get an A* in my ICT exam, only three marks off a perfect score, my E grade for my coursework dragged my final grade down to a C. Overall, not the worst outcome, and you could say that this situation wasn't entirely my fault, but looking back, there's a lot I could've done, had I cared a little more about my grade instead of checking social media every day and being able to get away with it. I could have contacted the head of the ICT department about my teacher. I could have worked harder on my database (not that it would've been correct, but I definitely could have still got a higher mark if I'd spent more than ten minutes a day on it). I could have looked up the grading criteria online and seen that we were all doing the wrong work – but I didn't. I was lazy, complacent, arrogant and assumed that I'd do well regardless.

However, whilst it would be easy for me to write off all of my experiences with teachers, I still believe at my core that the majority of people who work in the education sector do so because they love what they do. When I first began studying physics, I was given a pop quiz to assess my current skill level. To my shock and horror, I received an E. I remember sitting in my seat after the bell at the end of the school day had rung, tearful. My new teacher, Mr Harper, spotted me crying and came over.

'What's wrong?' he asked. When I explained how upset I was about getting one of the lowest scores out of my entire class he laughed, to my surprise.

'Don't be upset about it! It's the first physics lesson you've ever had! I promise you that your GCSE grade will be much higher by the time I'm through with you, okay? We'll make sure of it. Don't panic.'

Over the next two years, Mr Harper proved just how much he loved a challenge. Physics quickly became everyone's favourite lesson due to the way that he would teach us. He would treat us like adults, and not talk down to us like children. He would make lessons fun and interesting at the same time. Absolutely everyone in our class adored him, and by extension, wanted to learn as much as we could from him. By the time I took my final exam, I was able to give an answer to each and every question that came up in the paper. Physics ended up being the only subject for which I received an A* grade at GCSE, the highest grade possible. Mr Harper had taken me (as well as many others) from a low E grade and worked hard to make sure we all learned about physics because we wanted to, and not just because we had to. We all left that class with high grades. Bless you, Mr Harper.

I'm sure that if you've watched any of my videos on YouTube, you'll already be assuming what I was usually like at school. I'm someone who *loathes* being told what to do, to the point where reverse psychology is the easiest way to get me to do something. I would protest every order, roll my eyes and sigh, talk back like a smart-arse – and of course, that never went down well. I was often given detention for my attitude. There was one time when one of my teachers actually called for me to be stripped of my prefect tie because, despite him ordering me to sit away from my friend, I made it my mission to sit next to her at any opportunity I had out of sheer defiance. I was, to put it lightly, an arsehole. I was so swept up in trying to be funny and get a laugh from other kids in my classes that my education always came second – and whilst I didn't do badly at school, getting mostly As and Bs – those hours I spent being an arsehole mean nothing to me now, ten years on.

How cool you are to other people won't be relevant when you're an adult – nor will how unpopular you are, or how 'gross' you look. Your grades will stay with you for ever, and lead you on to bigger things: college, university, jobs. Sacrificing opportunities for temporary appearances just isn't worth it – I say that to you as the kid that didn't listen, and as the adult that would change an awful lot if she had the opportunity to go back and do it all again. This time around, the friends I had or didn't have wouldn't matter – homework wouldn't be put off until the last minute (I'm totally kidding, of course it would), and I would spend more of my free time in the school library, getting homework and coursework out of the way so I could enjoy my free time at home. Listen – the education system might be horrible, and it may (will) feel like a waste of your youth, but put the time in, buckle down, and reap the rewards – you'll thank yourself when you're older.

Teachers Are Human, Too

Oh man, teachers, amirite?! Such joyless, soulless human beings who seem intent on sucking out any fun you may be having talking to your friends, setting you homework when you've already got tons from your other classes, giving you detention when you don't do as you're told. That's how I used to think, anyway – teachers were the enemy, and I was the hero my school deserved, standing up to them at every opportunity and relishing the praise I'd get from my peers when I got sent out of class or given detention. The truth is (and this is something I only began to see as I started reaching the age that my teachers were when they were teaching me), regardless of how unfair you think your teachers are, they're still regular human beings with their own money problems, relationship woes and family issues – only with a pretty crappy job to boot. Imagine going to university, getting into thousands of pounds' worth of debt for a degree, only to be disrespected by kids all day instead of thanked for your hard work!

I'm not saying teachers are all wonderful, perfect people – they're human, therefore they can be arseholes – but even teachers are not immune to letting their personal problems get in the way of their work. No one is. There was a biology teacher in my school that everyone complained about. She gave out detentions like Oprah gave out cars, snapping and shouting at anyone who so much as dared to whisper something to a friend. We later found out that she was going through a rather messy divorce. Does that excuse how horrible she could be to some of her students? Of course not – but as someone who often got in trouble as a waitress for being grumpy over something that had happened *outside* of work, I can now completely understand why she was so ready to get angry at being disrespected.

Whilst this is a short section in this chapter, I felt as though it was needed – we are often slow to empathise when we feel as though we've been wronged, and we're happy to take our frustrations about more homework out on the person who gives it to us – but your teachers are just trying to do their job and help you succeed. If you and your entire class failed, they'd probably lose their jobs. Most teachers do what they do because they love it, and trust me, it's shitty pay too – and even though your day ends at 3.30 p.m., theirs goes on long into the night grading your papers. Do your part: ask yourself why teachers are asking you to be quiet and pay attention, try to understand that you having tons of homework in other subjects isn't their fault or problem, and, ultimately, remember that they're human. They're going to be tired, they're going to go through human emotions such as sadness and anger, and they'd probably really appreciate someone asking them, 'How are you?' for once.

The Social Circle

I'm gonna let you in on a little secret. Those kids that bitch about you in the corridor? In ten years' time, they won't be in your life. You may still casually hang out with a few people from your school when you're in your twenties, but you won't have to put up with the people you choose to leave behind every lunchtime like you would at school. I only kept in contact with one girl from my school who always showed me kindness – I still try to hang out with her as much as I can, and I love her to pieces. You can always decide to keep the friends you make in your life after school, but the ones you will leave behind are temporary. The people who are cruel to you aren't going to be relevant to you when you become independent – so why worry about what they think of you now?

At school, I was so concerned with getting everyone to like me. That's something I've battled with throughout my life. Despite being a short-tempered introvert, I always seek the approval of others. I dread the thought of anyone deciding that I'm a bad person, and at school, surrounded by over two hundred people exactly the same age as me, I was desperate to fit in at any cost. I flitted between friendship groups, changed my appearance and faked my music taste for five years – I flip-flopped between being someone who listened to pop and wore fake tan, and someone who had bright red hair, wore big, black baggy clothes and listened to metal. I answered back to teachers for a cheap laugh, getting myself in trouble to look cool. In trying to be someone I wasn't, nobody truly knew who I actually was – including myself. I ended up not being close to anyone for any extended period of time. In trying to fit in, I isolated myself from the people I wanted to like me.

Eventually, I found my stride as the class clown. If you've watched my YouTube channel, this may not surprise you. At some point during my teens, I discovered that I was pretty good at making others laugh, and decided to use it to my advantage – disrespecting teachers with witty comebacks, defacing desks with crude drawings and being sent out of class at least once a week for being disruptive. When I was fifteen, one of my teachers (who I really disliked, and those feelings were definitely mutual) caught me talking in class and asked me to repeat what she'd just said. Now, being anti-authority to the point where it's a problem (try telling me what to do. Let me know how that goes for you), I immediately snapped back, 'Sorry. I don't tend to listen to teachers like you.'

I got sent out of class, received a referral to our head of year and had to sit in detention for three lunchtimes for that.

Another example would be form time, when each morning and afternoon, we'd register our attendance with our form tutor and 'study' for twenty minutes. My form tutor, being a reasonable human, couldn't stand my insolence. Unfortunately for him, I'd also become extremely close to another girl in my form class, and we got on like a house on fire. The last thing a disruptive student should have is a partner in crime. Each and every form time, our form tutor would order my new best friend and me to sit at opposite ends of the classroom from one another in order to stop us being disruptive, and each and every form time, we would walk into the classroom and sit next to each other in an act of defiance. It basically became a running joke with our entire form class, and the only person who didn't find it funny was our form tutor. One afternoon, I walked through the door and immediately heard my form tutor bark, 'Emma, go to the head of year's office.'

I frowned.

'What? Why?' I asked.

'Because you're not going to be a prefect any more,' my tutor replied.

Oh yeah, that's the other thing that aggravated my teachers – despite being ... well, *a shit*, I was smart. I was in the top class for every subject, and mostly got the highest grades for any homework or exam. For that reason, I was made a prefect, adorned with a burgundy tie as opposed to a regular blue one. Somehow, I was someone the school trusted to set an example to the younger pupils (in truth, I just taught them how to burn books with hairspray and a lighter. Even though I wasn't popular with kids my own age, the younger kids liked me a *lot*).

I walked down the corridor towards our head of year's office, heart pounding. As much as I enjoyed being rebellious and getting a few cheap laughs, being a prefect was something I could put on my CV when I went out to get my first job – and how would I explain to my parents why my burgundy tie was gone? Suddenly, I felt a pang of regret for always being so rude to my teachers – were the few short sniggers I got occasionally from my peers worth it? The kids who laughed with me never actually chose to hang out with me outside class. Being disrespectful, as it turned out, didn't make me as many friends as I thought it did. Approaching the door to our head of year's office, I knocked quietly before stepping inside.

'Sir? You wanted to see me?' I asked sheepishly as Mr E gestured for me to sit down opposite him at his desk.

'Do you know why you're here?' he asked. I decided to feign ignorance.

'No, sir,' I replied. 'My form tutor just said I needed to come and see you.'

'I've had reports from him about your attitude,' Mr E said. 'And that made me go through your folder. Numerous detentions and referrals over the past year, all to do with your attitude and lateness . . . '

(Oh yeah. My new best friend and I also deliberately turned up late to morning registration. One morning, our form tutor asked us why we were late. I defiantly held up a bag of sweets we'd bought from the corner shop instead of walking to school. 'We got hungry,' I replied coolly, strolling over to my seat with a cocky swagger. I was an *actual dick*.)

'I don't know if you think you're being big, or clever . . . ' Mr E continued, looking over the pile of detention slips in front of him. 'But it's clear that you need to learn your lesson. I'm going to ask you to hand over your prefect tie.'

Now, whilst I did feel regret for how I'd acted, I'm . . . well, I'm dramatic, and I'm pretty good at getting things to swing my way. I turned on the waterworks.

'No, please, sir,' I sobbed. 'Things have been hard at home, I know I haven't been as well-behaved as I could have been . . . '

To my surprise, it worked! Mr E relented and allowed me to keep my prefect tie, on the condition that I worked on my behaviour. The look on my form tutor's face as he saw me waltz back into class still wearing my burgundy tie was one I'll never forget. I can only imagine words were had between my form tutor and Mr E afterwards.

This very real threat of having my prefect status stripped from me was enough to make me buck up my ideas, however. I knew all too well that I had found the boundary I was looking for when pushing my teachers, and for the final few months of secondary school, I stopped acting up in class and – for the most part – buckled down and focused on my studies and revision. I left school with mostly A grades, but I know that if I'd spent more time taking notes in class instead of looking for a way to make my peers snigger and think I was cool for a few seconds, I would have done even better. Do those few kids who thought I was funny remember me now? Do they remember my jokes, or my oh-so-cool attitude? Of course not! They're twenty-five, with jobs and kids. The only permanent reminder of school after you leave is the piece of paper telling you how well you did. That piece of paper helps you get on the career ladder, or into a good college or university. I'm speaking as someone who put the opinions of others ahead of my grades – in ten years' time, the people around you won't still be in your social circle. Perhaps one or two of them will, but the time you spend trying to impress your peers at school is a complete waste. You can't write on a CV, 'Yeah, but I made Jim in my biology class laugh once.'

As I've said, I spent a large amount of my time at school worrying about the opinions of my peers and trying to be liked. I was in and out of friendship groups as if they had a revolving door. I changed everything about myself a hundred times over, and out of those two hundred people in my school year, I only talk to one of them to this day. I also distinctly remember trying my hardest to follow the latest fashion trends with school uniform. In my school year, it was cool to have a tailored shirt that went *in* at the waist, and it had to be a couple of sizes too small to give you bigger boobs. You had to have a certain type of tight elasticated navy-blue trousers that had a cute little silver buckle sewn on them. And you had to have a miniature backpack that was so small you had to fold your exercise books in half to squash them in. Oh! And you *had* to defy the school rules and wear black trainers that could pass as smart black shoes. If you didn't do all these things, you were a nerd, a loser, you were *poor*, and you'd stick out like a sore thumb to the bullies.

I know this because I was a nerd, a loser, and I was poor, and I definitely stuck out like a sore thumb. I've spoken about bullies in previous chapters, but I was often mocked for my cheap blazer and stained tie because my family could only afford one of each; my long, baggy white shirt that had a chest pocket so big I could've snuck a hamster into school and no one would have known; my big, bulky black plastic shoes with huge rubber soles, and my big, oversized navy trousers that didn't have any type of cute buckle attached. I was dirty, I smelled a little, my skin and hair were constantly greasy because I grew up without a shower in our house (that's probably quite odd to many of you, but we only had a bathtub and couldn't afford to get a shower installed), and I was sort of known as one of the least 'well-off' kids in my year. Each and every lunchtime, I strategically worked out which corridors I could go down and which ones I should avoid if I didn't want to bump into the group of vicious girls that would make fun of me, and each and every night I begged my dad to buy me the tight-fitting clothes and trainers that would mean I would be left alone.

'For the last time, we can't afford it,' my dad would groan, clearly annoyed at my lack of gratitude for the things he managed to buy for me through scrimping and saving. I remember being so angry – if only I had those trousers, the bullies would leave me alone, and people would stop sitting away from me in class, and people might think I was cool . . .

I don't speak to any of those people I once tried to impress. Sometimes I look them up on Facebook just out of curiosity. They're all adults, with jobs and babies, and wouldn't remember my name if it was written on the front cover of a book and flung at their faces. My point is that for all the complaining I did about my social status at school, it is completely irrelevant to my life now. When you're at school, being liked can feel like the *be all and end all*. Being popular – or at least, not having people tease you – can feel like priority *numero uno*, and can often overtake your desire to do well in your studies. I urge you to remember that friends come and go, but the grades you leave with are for ever. In ten years' time, your souvenirs from school will consist only of your grades and the people you choose to keep around.

This goes for being bullied, too. I wish I'd had the attitude of, 'In a few years, you'll be out of my life, and you won't matter to me,' when I was being teased and desperate for approval, because then that crushing feeling of humiliation and rejection wouldn't have felt anywhere near as bad. The second you step out of that school building on your final day, you're no longer forced to be around the kids that make your life a misery – you are free to drop them, and suddenly, every opinion they had of you will be irrelevant. Spend your time and energy working hard, taking notes, doing your homework, and try to spend less time worrying about what people think of you. Work and act as though they are already out of your life. You'll thank yourself in ten years' time.

Best Friends, Bitching And Bullying

Here's the life lesson I want to put across to you here, without any extra waffle: if you hear someone bitching and gossiping about someone, *don't join in*. If you hear someone making up a lie about someone, be bold, correct them, and *don't join in*. If someone is bitching about somebody else and asks you what you think about them, *remain neutral*, even if you do have a negative opinion. Do not start bitching. Do not start gossiping. Do not spread lies about people. Do not be mean about others online, even if you think you're anonymous. Speak no evil, and your school life – no, your *life in general* – will be less dramatic, less complicated, and you'll find yourself in a lot fewer confrontations, and in a lot less trouble.

My first story is pretty short, but I think it's a good example of how things can very quickly get out of hand when you're caught bitching about someone behind their back. It takes place during my second year of college. I was seventeen, and still trying to get over the relationship with Ben (remember him? First love? Shitty band?) that had ended a few months earlier. Ben was happy and in love with Jasmine (remember her? Cool, pretty indie kid who is now my friend because we bond over how much of a shithead Ben was?) and I still had to witness the two of them holding hands and kissing in the corridors, my heart breaking as I slowly began to accept that Ben and I wouldn't be getting back together. I hated Jasmine. I *hated* her. In my mind, she'd stolen my first love. If she wasn't around, Ben would have got back with me and we would've been *happy*. Of course, this would never have been the case, but ah, to be young and naive again.

During the summer holidays between my first and second year of college, I was sitting on Twitter having a conversation with a friend, when suddenly, he made a mean joke indirectly referencing Jasmine. We began to tweet back and forth something along the lines of:

Friend: Well, at least you're not stuck up like some people . . .

Me: Look at me! I'm so indie! I love The Beach Boys! I'm so cool!!

The tweets went back and forth, indirectly mocking Jasmine. I was angry, and knew that despite her not following me on Twitter, she'd see the tweets. I wanted her to know how much I hated her. I wanted her to feel awful for dating the love of my life. I wanted her to be upset. She *deserved* it.

Needless to say (honestly, I hope it's obvious) she *didn't* deserve it. The tweets my friend and I sent were a pure example of cyber-bullying, although my tweets were a lot worse than his. I sent the tweets with the intention of upsetting her, because they were *obviously* going to get back to her – and after a few minutes, the satisfaction of tweeting about Jasmine died away, and I deleted the tweets, thinking nothing more of it.

On my first day back at college, in my first ICT lesson of the year, a note was passed from the office to my teacher. I had been summoned to see the head of our college year. Confused, I did as I was told. I made my way to the head of year's office, knocked on the door, just as I'd done in school over my prefect tie, and let myself in.

'You wanted to see me?' I asked politely, with no idea why I was being asked to take a seat. My head of year sat there, stony-faced, and without saying a word, placed her hand on some printed sheets of paper and spun them round for me to read. There, in front of me, were screenshots of every tweet I'd sent to my friend about Jasmine. Every nasty, vicious word, staring me in the face, and the immediate shame I felt for what I'd written washed over me. My head of year pulled the sheets away from me and back towards her, before reading out each and every one, painstakingly slowly. My cheeks burned a furious red. The words being read back to me sounded as though they were from a completely different person – a nasty, horrible one who enjoyed making others upset – and then I realised that this was exactly what I'd become.

It turns out that Jasmine had seen the tweets, and had been in tears for an entire day before telling her mum, who then demanded that I be punished for what I'd said. I was threatened with expulsion from college, but fortunately I was told that, if I wrote a handwritten apology to Jasmine, I wouldn't be expelled. I wrote my apology (and it was heartfelt, too – I genuinely felt awful for what I'd done) and was allowed to stay. After that, Jasmine and I kept a mutual, civil distance from each other for the rest of our time at college, only truly reconciling at a gig a year later, and, well, you know the rest. Jasmine and Ben broke up, Ben tried to win me back whilst he was still dating her, and we often bond over his shitty, desperate behaviour. As for the tweets? We don't really ever talk about it, but she knows how much I regret what I did, and chose to forgive me for it.

I refuse to sugarcoat it: I was a cyber-bully, plain and simple. I was immature and acting out of jealousy of her happiness with the ex I still cared for, and said nasty things with the intention of upsetting her in the public domain. I have absolutely no excuse for that, and I own it completely. To this day, ever since I realised the impact I'd had on Jasmine and on the future of my education, I have refused to participate in cyber-bullying – only ever calling out people when they have wronged a friend, but without spitting venom and using name-calling as a weapon.

As I've got older and (slightly) wiser, I've begun to read over any incensed online posts before publishing them, wondering if they'd hurt and upset someone in a way I didn't intend. If I have a problem with a friend or colleague, I will do my best to talk to them in a calm manner in private looking to resolve our issues. Some people will do anything they can to 'stir the pot' – sometimes out of malice, sometimes just out of boredom. It never ends well. Getting caught up in the rumour mill and resorting to bitching and name-calling will only ever have a negative outcome that will outweigh the temporary feeling of satisfaction you'll get from venting about someone, and the easiest way to avoid that negative outcome is to simply refuse to participate.

You may feel that, if you don't join in with bitching and gossiping, your friends will think you're standing up for the people they hate, and it'll affect your friendship. If that's how you feel about your friends, they're not your friends. Nobody should encourage you to spread rumours or talk badly about someone. If a person has upset your friend and you hear them venting about how *horrible and ugly* they are, it may be best to keep quiet, nod and try to comfort your friend in a way that isn't joining in on their rant. If someone has wronged you and you cannot calmly talk to them about it, write down your feelings, no matter how cruel, on a piece of paper, and tear it up into little pieces once you're done so that no one can find it. I often find that after venting to a piece of paper, those angry feelings for that person I'm upset with fade away as I rip it up and throw it away. If I'd done that instead of doing what I decided to do to Jasmine on Twitter, I wouldn't have cyber-bullied someone to the extent of almost being expelled from college.

Never act on impulse. Think about the impact your words can have (and actions too – even standing by and laughing about someone behind their back is as cruel as the words you're laughing at) and try to resolve your issues calmly. Be diplomatic, use your words, and you'll be able to dedicate more of your time to the people you like instead of to the people that you're upset with. Isn't that a better use of our time?

You Can Only Do Your Best

Rarely is there a pressure bigger than the one you put on yourself to achieve and succeed. Of course, pressure from parents who want you to get straight As and become a lawyer or a doctor is horrid (thankfully, I never experienced that), and pressure from teachers to get a perfect grade when they don't seem to take into account the workload you have in other subjects is enough to put the calmest person on edge, but the fear of letting yourself down in an aspect of your life that you care about is unparalleled. The pressure you put on yourself will continue long after you've left school. As you get older, you'll become all too aware that life is short and you only have a set amount of years to make something of yourself. It's pretty much inescapable until something *clicks* in your brain (it tends to happen after forty, apparently. I'll have to let you know) and you no longer put pressure on yourself to achieve every dream you ever had.

However, I have been very fortunate to have an incredible father in my life who ensured that one phrase was drummed into me from a very young age: *You can only do your best.*

Realistically, there is only so much revision you can do before you can no longer concentrate. There is only so much your brain can take in. There'll be some things that just won't make any sense. For instance, I have never, ever been able to do long division. Every other kid in my maths classes could do long division without even thinking about it – carrying the remainder, dropping numbers down . . . and I just couldn't do it. Still can't. For the longest time, I was so insecure about being the only kid that didn't get it, I would get really upset. I would feel stupid, and put so much pressure on myself to get it right, to the point where I was on the verge of tears when my dad tried to calmly explain the steps over and over again. This wasn't when I was nine or ten years old, this was when I was sixteen!

Sometimes you might feel as though your best isn't good enough – and when we're fed the 'You can do anything you set your mind to' line so many times, that reality can be heartbreaking – but what else can you do? My dad always said to me that so long as I put my everything into a task, he couldn't ask me for more, and because of that, I never felt pressure to achieve more than what was possible for me. Of course, if I didn't at least try, that was cause for disappointment – from my dad and from myself – but you can only ever do your best. Your best is good enough because you are trying your utmost with everything you have. Remember that.

I was twenty years old the first time I attempted wrestling training. (Yes, I wanted to be a professional wrestler, because professional wrestling is fucking cool.) I'd joined a gym a few weeks prior, doing my best to increase my fitness levels in preparation for the lessons. I walked into the wrestling school, my heart filled with excitement at the prospect of finally taking steps towards achieving my dream – and then I was given my first suplex. If you don't know what a suplex is, it's a wrestling move where you are picked up from behind and thrown down on to your back. Wrestling, as it turns out, is not as 'fake' as some would have you believe. It *hurts*. I walked (limped) away from my first lesson in disbelief at how much wrestling demands from the body. I felt in my heart that I simply couldn't pursue this dream. I was crushed. However, after a short while, I realised that I didn't need to be a wrestler to work in the wrestling business. There are plenty of roles within the industry that I could fill if I wished to pursue them that I would enjoy just as much (and experience a lot less pain whilst doing so). I could be a backstage presenter, a social media manager for the wrestlers, a production assistant – it is all about exploring different ways to go about your dreams.

I decided to try my hand at professional wrestling again at the age of twenty-five – because when I say 'give it your all', I practise what I preach – and I quickly remembered the pain and demand for extreme fitness. If I truly wanted to go for it, I know I would have fought through the pain, but going by the fact that I've given up twice, I know that wrestling isn't truly my dream job. If it was, I know I would stop at nothing to achieve it.

Just make sure that no matter what you are trying to do – whether that's passing an exam, applying for a job or trying to break into an industry – you give nothing less than your very best. Do not be afraid to make mistakes, as you will learn from them. You owe it to yourself to keep trying your very best and giving everything one hundred and ten per cent – if you don't, you'll only have yourself to answer to.

As much as I've said that your school grades are the most important thing about school – and they *are* – if you try your hardest at an exam and still don't get the grade you wanted, it can be crushing. Listen, this isn't going to sound like the most tragic example in the world, but at school, I *loved* studying English Language. I loved creative writing, and my coursework for the subject got the highest mark available (I literally got a perfect score – I'm not too sure this book will reflect that . . .). I was a smug little bastard (that's not a surprise, is it?) and being the 'smartest' (statistically speaking) kid in my class made me feel so much pride in my writing ability that I walked into my exam cocky as all hell. I was going to ace it – only the writing segment was something I hadn't anticipated. It wasn't asking me to write a short story, but a piece of journalism based on an excerpt we hadn't received before the test. I was stunned. I gave it my all, determined to get the highest grade I could, but I was suddenly shaken. I had been so confident that I would get the highest grade imaginable, just as I had with my coursework, and now I was being asked to write completely out of my comfort zone.

When I received my exam result back a few months later, I was devastated. I'd been predicted an A* all the way through my two-year GCSE course, had been revered by my teachers as a teenage prodigy, a future best-selling author (lol) – and I got an A. To make matters worse (without thinking) my disappointed teacher, who had believed in my abilities from the start, told me that the minimum mark I'd needed to get an A* was 134 marks . . . and I'd got 133. I was one mark away from an A*. I was fuming, I was hurt, and I was utterly disappointed with myself. I had let myself down. If only I'd anticipated a journalistic piece, I could have studied for that style of writing, and not let my exam drag down my perfect coursework grade.

For *years*, this mark stayed on my mind. What if I'd studied harder? What if I'd written differently? Even now as I write this (as an author . . . weird, that) I remember that burning, bitter disappointment I felt when I found out I was one mark away. However, that grade wasn't the end of the world. I still did incredibly well! I still got my first job, I still got into college, and my heart kept on beating, and most of all I did the best that I could with what

I had. Life will sometimes deal you an unfair hand. You will feel cheated, or perhaps you will feel as though you have screwed up somewhere along the line – but I know now that during that exam, despite my situation, I did the best that I could. I couldn't have tried harder in those sixty short minutes, and in that respect, I achieved a lot.

Equally, there were exams that I didn't do well in because I didn't try hard at all – I got a C in GCSE electronics, as well as a U in A level maths, because my heart simply wasn't in those subjects. The disappointment I felt in myself for not trying as hard as I could burned more then than it did over the English Language exam, where I tried my hardest. If you don't try as hard as you can, you will always think to yourself, *What if? What if I'd tried harder? What if I'd tried at all . . . ?* If you *do* try your hardest there is no way you can possibly think that.

There have been times I have been turned down for jobs, or seen a video that I worked hard on not get the views I'd hoped for – but as long as you try as hard as you possibly can, you can walk away with your head held high. I did everything I could, you can say to yourself in your failure. There was nothing I could have done differently with what I was given. I can only ever do my best. My best is all I can give – and my best is good enough.

9

You Better Werk It

Getting A Job

Contrary to popular belief (or at least, the belief of my nastiest online critics) I do have experience of the 'real world' – in a world filled with headlines such as 'Teenage YouTube Sensation Earns SEVEN MILLION DOLLARS A YEAR!' it's easy to see those who make a living from posting online as naive idiots who have never had a 'real job'. I very much *have* had 'real jobs' (if we're assuming what I do for a living now is somehow *not* real?) and I've been chewed up and spat out from many different rungs of the career ladder. Despite my latter jobs all being based in the hospitality sector (I was a waitress. 'Working in hospitality' sounds much better), my first job, if you remember, was a weekend position in a big shoe shop in my home town. I'd just turned sixteen, but had been handing out my CV for almost a year in the hope that it would be kept on file. I don't know whether it was down to my clearly impeccable skills at writing a CV (if you couldn't tell already, I'm not bad at bigging myself up. My CV basically equated to me saying 'Listen, hire me, because I'm the absolute tits'), or whether it was luck, but I've never really had an issue with at least getting a callback after handing in a CV to a place with a vacancy, and I suppose I'm good at face-to-face interviews. However, when I was sixteen, with only GCSE predictions (having not even taken my exams at this point), I knew that applying for a job in the shoe shop would probably be an unsuccessful venture. This shoe shop practically relied on school kids to run it on the weekends, and the shop would get an average of ten CVs a day. However, due to my impeccable CV-writing skills (and if you recall, probably also due to the pastel blue paper I printed mine on), I got a callback, and after a short interview, I got the job. That's my tip for you if you're going for a job where your qualifications can't put you ahead of others – print your CV on blue paper. Works like a charm.

Oh, and it's all about *how* you word your CV. For the record, I can't tell you to fake your exam results on a CV, because that would be **abhorrent**, even if they never actually ask to see them. I can't tell you to get your mum to pretend to be a teacher when your potential employer asks for a reference. I'd never tell you to pretend your hobbies include archery, horseback riding, abseiling and volunteering at a local charity shop because you just love working so damn much. That would be **irresponsible**, and even if those things *did* help you get your first job, I am an **incredibly excellent role model** and would never tell any of you to *lie to get a job*.

Anyway . . . there are certain words that you might be tempted to use when asked to describe yourself, and you won't be the only

person using them. Don't say 'hard-working'. Everyone says that.
Say 'dedicated' or 'committed to giving one hundred and ten per
cent to helping my team excel'. And don't say 'reliable'. Nothing
says 'I'm not actually reliable' more than saying 'I am reliable'. If
you really were reliable, you wouldn't have to say it. Same with
'honest'. You're basically saying, 'I'm not a thief, but even if I
were, I wouldn't write it here.' Talk about your personality! Say
you're 'athletic' or 'energetic'. That tells your employer you're
good at running around like a blue-arsed fly and completing
tasks quickly. Hell, just go all out and write 'I'm good at running
around like a blue-arsed fly and completing tasks quickly'. The
shock factor sometimes works. Talk about your sense of humour.
Hey, if you're feeling really confident (also, absolutely make sure
you write the word 'confident', because that's a *super word* for
employers), then start your CV with a joke. There's definitely a
fine line between 'confident' and 'arrogant' though. Remember
you don't have a rapport with the stranger reading your CV for
the first time – they can't see your face, they can't read things in
your voice – so keep things natural and non-intimidating. Don't
write too much about yourself, but don't make yourself look
vapid and boring. Here's an example of what I would write on a
CV about myself now (and don't just copy it word for word, for
crying out loud . . .).

Personal qualities: Outgoing, light-hearted, confident of my ability to put smiles on the faces of everyone I meet. Energetic and
dedicated to putting one hundred and ten per cent effort into
everything I do. Fast-learner who takes pride in leaving no job
unfinished. Hobbies include competitive badminton, cycling and

studying global current affairs. Strongest qualities include pride in my consistently positive attitude, cleanliness and a good sense of humour (well, apparently . . .).

Doesn't that sound better than 'I'm a hard worker who is punctual and friendly. Hobbies include networking and listening to music'? That's a good point, by the way – don't think employers don't know what 'networking' means. It means you tweet. After a while, I was put in charge of handling CVs in the department store café, and we were told to immediately throw away any CVs that didn't look good enough. I'm not sure that was company policy, but even when we'd say, 'We'll keep it on file,' we most likely didn't. Make your CV stand out, because it will be skim-read before employers decide whether or not to keep it.

Now – am I outgoing, as I wrote in my example CV? Am I energetic? Do I give one hundred and ten per cent effort to everything I do? Do I play 'competitive badminton'?! Do I fuck! However, I do think I have an okay sense of humour, and I do study 'global current affairs' (meaning I have a weird fascination with books and documentaries about North Korea, but imagine writing that?). It's all in the wording. An employer can't prove you don't cycle, or that you're not energetic, until you've already got the job. They don't know if you leave jobs unfinished or not. They take a chance on you – and if you come across in your CV as someone who is confident enough to lie to their faces about how great you are, the chances are, they'll believe you.

Of course, if you *are* all those things, and you *are* smart, and *do* have experience, well, this chapter is wasted on you. However, that doesn't necessarily mean you'll get every job you apply for.

Rejection can really burn if you let it, because it leaves you with unanswered questions. *Why wasn't I good enough? What did other applicants have that I didn't? Did I come across badly?* Dealing with any rejection can make you feel inadequate, but each rejection is a life lesson. Perhaps you were nervous in the interview, or perhaps there was just someone better suited to the job. That doesn't mean you're not worthy of employment, and it doesn't mean you're useless – dust yourself off and try again. Tweak your CV every now and then. Try for jobs you weren't originally aiming for just to earn some more experience. After being rejected a few times, you can start to feel hopeless, but I'm a firm believer in, 'If you try, you might fail. If you don't try, you'll *definitely* fail.'

Also, if your interviewer asks which place you play badminton at, make it up and don't return their calls.

It's Just A Job

From the moment we're old enough to comprehend what a 'job' is, we're taught to understand that being employed is a sacred, golden opportunity – money is what allows us to live. Money can be exchanged for goods and services! Money is how we become happy. Jobs allow you to *make* that money. However – it is important that we do not allow ourselves to be tricked into thinking that only by having a job and earning money can we be happy. Of course, I'm not prepared to go on record saying, 'Jobs suck! Quit your job! Be unemployed on purpose!' As you know, I was in and out of different jobs right the way up until I was twenty-one, when I was able to earn enough from YouTube to sustain a decent living.

For the entire time I was in professional employment, be it selling shoes, serving fries or waiting tables, I felt fortunate to have a job, and I was absolutely terrified of being fired. If you're fired, any future employer will call up your last place of work and find out, right? What if you suddenly can't find another job and then have to explain why you've been out of employment for months? All of these imaginary worst-case scenarios turned me into a complete and utter doormat when it came to being bossed around. My feelings were at their worst when I was working at the department store café for two years. Any time I was asked to cover someone's shift, I would immediately agree, out of fear of being seen as 'undependable' and being fired if I didn't. I would end up working an hour or two of overtime almost each and every day, often unpaid. I agreed to come in early whenever I was asked, whether it was on a late shift, on days off or on any bank holiday that other colleagues refused to work. Whenever I did something wrong, or snapped at a customer (work in retail – it happens), and was called up for a disciplinary hearing, I was terrified that the store manager (who I felt *hated* me) would find a way to fire me. I became a miserable, beaten-down wreck. A slave to the wage, a rat in a cage, feeling unable to say no to working six or seven days a week and leaving myself no time to look for another job. Besides, the company had done a good enough job of convincing me that I was lucky to still *have* a job after being so bad at it, and that I should feel grateful in our fragile economy to be employed. Of course, that was partly true – I wasn't a model employee – but this gradual brainwashing into believing my life would crumble without this job made me so dependent on it that I would hate waking up in the mornings.

Every night, I would come home, change out of my uniform, eat dinner and tell my dad about my day. He would shake his head in despair.

'I don't get why you won't just quit,' he would say. 'It's just a job.'

'Well, what would I do if I quit, Dad?' I would snap back, close to tears. 'I can't quit! I need to earn money!'

'Yes, you need the money. Yes, you need a job,' he would argue, almost pleading with me. 'But if you're going to come home every night and complain and sit there in tears, you should at least be looking for another job! You're doing nothing about it!'

This was also true of my time at the fast food restaurant when I was eighteen, working weekend shifts while I was at college. Every Saturday morning, my dad would drive me to the restaurant, and he would have to sit and watch me almost break down in tears, my stomach churning with anxiety due to the stress of the job and the bully that I had for a manager – more about her later.

It really wasn't until I was able to break the cycle and become my own boss that I realised how downtrodden I'd truly been. Again, this is not to say I think you should all quit your jobs – but merely realise that your employer cannot get away with as much as you might let them. For instance, I would often volunteer to work extra shifts at the café – not because I wanted to, and not even for the extra money. I did it because I was afraid that by saying no I would be fired, or anger my bosses and get another black mark against my record, giving them more ammo to use in order to fire me later on down the line. My job was my life. I was doing all the roles that a supervisor would do (and often,

I acted as the role of 'manager' when my own boss was taking a day off) and still being paid the same wage as my colleagues with far fewer responsibilities. I was overworked, underpaid and depressed. The feeling of being trapped and at the bottom of the pecking order often made me lash out at customers, leading to more disciplinary hearings, which then led to me working even harder in order to avoid being fired. If I'd known then what I know now, I would have refused the hours I didn't need – there is no way you can be fired for not taking extra hours, so long as you still complete your minimum weekly hours as per your contract. You'll never be fired if you abide by the rules of your workplace. Anything that goes above and beyond what you're contracted for is optional. I also would have demanded a pay rise to match the wage of a supervisor, or else I would have refused to carry out supervisor tasks such as audits, stock orders, break delegation and till overrides. Most importantly of all, when I was sitting opposite the store manager's desk, shaking with fear at being chastised for something small as she threatened to file a disciplinary hearing against my record, I would've said to myself, 'It's just a job.'

Again, and I'm getting sick of writing it, I'm not saying jobs aren't important. We have an economy to run! We have bills to pay! However – losing your job doesn't mean it's the end of the world. Of course, it would be stressful (I have actually been fired from a job and the worry on your mind *sucks*) but for me, the toll that was being taken on my mental health in order for me to stay in my bosses' 'good books' simply wasn't worth it. As an employee, you have certain rights, and your managers know it. If they breach those rights, challenge them on it. Take it higher to head office if you need to. Do not let any employer make you feel scared for your future in order to get you to do more than you're being paid for. If you do, this is your message telling you to jump ship. Look for a company that will value you as an employee.

Would I ever go back to working for someone else? Sure. Only next time around, I'll be equipped with the knowledge of my rights. I'll know what I can and can't be fired for. I'm not the doormat I was five years ago. From now on, I will only work somewhere that makes me feel valued and respected. No amount of money will make me stay somewhere that beats me down. After all, yes, we need money to live, and I was lucky not to have a lot of mouths to feed (and I was still living at home) but ultimately, it's like my dad tried to tell me throughout my time of being bullied, trodden on and threatened with being fired when I legally couldn't be: 'It's just a job.'

High School Never Ends

At my school, whenever I or a fellow classmate would protest to our teacher about homework or our uniforms, we were always met with the same response: 'School has these rules in order to prepare you for the workplace.'

Have you ever heard a teacher say that? I'm starting to wonder whether or not this phrase was pinned up on a memo board in the staff room for my teachers to recite like zombies during lunch-times. However, they kind of had a point – whilst it was hard to make those comparisons whilst I was still *at* school, the similarities between school and work become increasingly obvious after a few years in employment:

- ↯ You have to go to a place you don't really want to go to.

- ↯ You have to wear a uniform you don't really want to wear.

- ↯ You have to meet deadlines for things that seem unnecessary.

- ↯ Your peers can be dicks.

- ↯ Your superiors can be dicks.

- ↯ You can be bullied by either class of dick.

I've spoken already about some of the experiences of bullying I had at school, and I also stressed the importance of not allowing a bully to ruin your school life – after all, once you leave, they're out of your life, right? However, just as with school, the more ruthless workplaces will have a social circle from which you can most definitely be excluded, and they can be filled with gossiping and bullies – but in the very worst of them, the bullies are your superiors.

I've spoken already about my supervisor 'Mel' from the shoe shop. She was the one who stood toe-to-toe with me on the shop floor over some stupid email forms for a newsletter, but in the grand scheme of things, she wasn't actually in charge. She didn't run the day-to-day operations of the store and there was nothing she could really do to mess with me. However, at the helm of that same shoe shop stood the store manager, who had the attitude of a pissed-off grandma. She had been running the store for over ten years, and from the second I met her at my job interview, she gave me the heebie-jeebies. If you've seen the film *Matilda,* she was comparable to Miss Trunchbull (I'm fairly sure my fellow teenage weekend employee and I actually referred to her as 'Trunchbull' when we knew we could get away with it). For the most part, she didn't work on weekends. However, on the Saturdays and Sundays that she did work, or whenever I agreed to work on a weekday to earn more money during school holidays, I was in constant fear of doing something wrong. This store manager had both the bark *and* the bite, snapping at anyone who was standing around for more than five seconds, berating employees in front of customers if they weren't selling enough shoe spray or if they weren't getting enough email addresses for the newsletter. Compared to her, Mel was like a best friend.

Whilst our store manager believed in equality (by which I mean she spared no employee from her wrath when we weren't meeting our targets), there was something she did towards the end of my time at the shoe shop that was far beyond what could be deemed acceptable. I'd been working there since late 2007 (just after my sixteenth birthday) and a year into my employment, in the summer of 2008, I kindly requested that my holiday dates (none of which I'd taken up until this point out of sheer *terror*) be over the August Bank Holiday so that I could attend a music festival with my then-boyfriend 'Ben'. I knew the store manager wasn't going to be best pleased. August Bank Holiday was the 'back to school' weekend, when hordes of frantic parents would swarm to the store in order to buy some last-minute school shoes for little Jimmy, whose feet had grown six sizes over the summer. There was an unspoken, informal rule that every employee was to be on standby over this weekend and called to work when necessary. However – it wasn't in any part of our contracts that we had to be available. After some convincing from my dad to 'just do it, stop being afraid all the time', I left my request in writing and put it on the store manager's desk on Sunday evening, a month before the August Bank Holiday. A month's notice! Surely a whole month is a respectable amount of notice in order for my manager to prepare for one pair of hands being absent for that weekend?

On Monday evening after school, I received a call on my mobile from the store's number.

'Hello?'

'Hello, is this Emma?' my store manager barked, knowing full well it was me.

'Yes, speaking . . .'

'This is [Trunchbull]. I've just read your request for a holiday over the August Bank Holiday. As you know, no one's allowed that weekend off. If you can't be available, you're going to have to hand in your notice.'

Hand in my notice?! Was I being fired? Was this even legal?!

'I'm sorry, [Trunchbull], but it's the weekend of the music festival I've had planned for months.'

'Right, okay. Come into the store and hand in your notice tomorrow.' *Click.* My store manager hung up the phone. Bear in mind I was sixteen years old, and this was my first job. I burst into tears and ran downstairs to tell my dad, sobbing.

'She can't do that,' my dad said, outraged. 'That's not legal! She can't fire you for that. Don't hand in your notice, she'll get over it.'

I wiped away my tears, praying my dad was right. Only, the next evening, another phone call.

'Hello?'

'Emma? Hi, it's [Trunchbull]. Just calling to see when you're going to hand in your notice so I can hire someone who actually wants a job.'

My manager had called my mobile out of work hours once again – and she did the same thing the next night. In the end, I was a mess, stressed from the thought of confrontation and the punishment that I would receive during every shift if I didn't resign – and so I gave in. On Thursday evening after school, against my dad's best pleas, I handed in my two weeks' notice of resignation to the supervisor on duty, worked the next two weeks alongside the young girl who would be replacing me, and left. I went to the music festival, had an amazing time, and then returned home to face the fact that I no longer had a part-time job, and there would be a gap on my CV for all future employers to see.

Now, there may be some of you reading this particular story who will side with my store manager – she wanted me to quit so that she could hire someone who could be there for that weekend. However, regardless of what you think about my desire to go to a music festival, I believe what she did was *not* legal, and called 'constructive dismissal'. Due to the fact that I had not broken any rules within my contract, my manager couldn't legally fire me, despite her best efforts.

Hindsight is always 20/20 – and if I'd known then what I know now (another saying that I've found myself repeating increasingly often) there is no way in *hell* I would've quit the way I did! At the age of twenty-five, I wouldn't have answered my manager's calls out of hours. I wouldn't have handed in my notice, and pressed for my manager to accept my notice for that weekend off. I would have quoted my contract like gospel. I would have gone to head office, to hell with the consequences. I would have kept my job, like the megalith for stubbornness I have become, in spite of feeling any pressure – and would have found another job on my own terms, and in my own time. If conditions at the workplace had become unbearable in the lead-up to me quitting, I would have taken them to court. Read up on what your boss can and cannot get away with – you have a right not to be harassed or forced out of your job.

Unfortunately, my experience with my superiors didn't improve going into my next job. In fact, they got much worse.

Somehow, I survived almost a year at the fast food restaurant. To this day, this goes down in my own history as the worst job I ever had. This particular chain's system seemed based on gender – young and pretty teenage girls working the tills facing customers, and the males of any age working in the kitchen. At seventeen years old, for my first shift, I was immediately put to work on the tills . . . on a Saturday morning. Fast food restaurants are hell on Saturday mornings. Without any training on the till whatsoever, I was told to take over another employee's till account and begin taking orders, without making any mistakes (the store would only be allowed a few till refunds per day, and if you made too many mistakes, you would be fired for incompetence), with the aim of completing any order within ninety seconds. Needless to say, I had to ask for help finding every single menu item on the massive system, shaking as I apologised to the waiting customers.

'Excuse me, Heather, where is this burger, I'm sorry ...' I stuttered, turning round to face the shift manager, who was scowling at me.

'For fuck's sake,' she spat, slamming down the customer's drink on to the tray before proceeding to jab buttons on the screen in front of me. 'Look, burgers, savers, no cheese, done. Fucking useless.'

As she walked away, I stood there in shock, quickly looking down with bright red cheeks and taking the customer's cash. Despite all that my shoe-store manager had put me through, she had never sworn at me or called me useless. As I once again struggled to find another menu item, Heather barged me out of the way.

'Fuck's sake, I'll just do it, shall I?' she hissed, immediately taking over the till duties with a big smile on her face for the customers.

'Okay ...' I said, close to tears. 'What do you want me doing?'

'I don't care, just go and do something else.'

I walked away, cheeks burning with shame as Heather took over, her eyes not meeting my gaze as I looked back at her. Truth be told, at this point I was just relieved to be away from her – but without any instructions, I walked around the restaurant, at a loss what to do. Over the next few shifts, Heather would put me back on the tills at busy times but being new, and only being assigned to them on Saturday mornings, I would never be able to fully grasp how the system worked. Eventually, I was assigned to cleaning duties, and keeping the restaurant tidy became my main task until I was able to get a new job.

However – it felt to me like Heather had already decided that she did not like me, no matter how busy or quiet the restaurant was. She would ignore me at every opportunity, talking over me when I asked to go on a break, only really acknowledging my presence by barking at me or ordering me to do a task that was completely demoralising. One of my worst memories of the restaurant is being ordered to clean the dirt in between the tiles with a small, wooden coffee stirrer – right underneath her feet. On other occasions, I would be sent to stand outside to greet customers – rain or shine. Whenever I would start my shift and find out she was the shift manager, my stomach would lurch. I felt it was always me who got the grossest, most demoralising tasks, and as soon as I was able to put my feet up, she would bark at me to finish my lunch break as early as I could, meaning I only really had five minutes to shovel down a quick burger before heading back out to clean tables. Whenever my shift was over, I would need to ask her if I could go. I remember countless times when she would refuse to let me clock out and made me leave my dad sitting outside in his car while I did another disgusting job before being allowed to go.

However, as time went on and I began to befriend my co-workers, I realised that her antics weren't doing her any favours – absolutely no one had a kind word to say about her, and she was always left out when it came to social events outside work. Eventually my colleagues from the kitchen, who had worked there a lot longer than me, began to stand up for me, telling Heather to let me go home at the correct time and take my lunch breaks. With their support giving me the confidence I so sorely needed, I began to tell her that it was the end of my shift and leaving before she could stop me, instead of merely asking for her permission. I began to take my full break which I was entitled to, and often just stayed out of her sight so that she couldn't find something disgusting for me to do. As soon as I was able to leave college and look for a full-time job, I left to work in the department store café and never returned.

Working at the fast food restaurant was the worst job experience I've ever had, and it was only when I started to gain confidence in my abilities that I began to treat my time there as more of a job than a punishment.

The moral of this story is that, ultimately, there will be superiors that try to assert their power over you – but bullying in the workplace is illegal, and nobody at your place of work, boss or not, has the right to make you feel pathetic or inferior to them. If you have a difficult boss, report their behaviour to their own superiors, and if the job isn't your passion, look for a new one as soon and as often as you can if no action is taken. In the meantime, stand your ground – if there is a task you're not trained for, you can refuse to do it. If there is a job you feel violates health and safety (such as unblocking a customer toilet with just a pair of gloves – yes, I was asked to do that), then you can and should refuse to do it. Bullies are only bullies whilst they can get away with it – whether that's at school or in the workplace. Stay strong, remember that you are not the problem, and don't let anyone make you feel inferior without your consent.

10

Self-Worth

You Are A Miracle

I'm not gonna spend too long on this part, but I want to remind you that the chances of you *coming to be* in this universe were so small, so immeasurable, that the fact that you *are* here, as you are, is nothing short of a miracle. I'm not trying to push a religious agenda on to you here – take the word 'miracle' as you will – but whether you believe it's by coincidence or by design, there is a reason you are unique, and that there will never be another human exactly like you (unless you want to bring up identical twins, in which case, you're really reaching here. I'm trying to make you feel special, for fuck's sake).

Let's get a little gross. You know how babies are made, right? If not, well . . . go and ask your parents and then come back. I'll wait.

Great! You're back! Sorry you had to find out the gross stuff. You know during that . . . *act of creation*, you were one of *billions* that could've turned into a baby, right? Each one of those billions of candidates would have turned out differently to you, and had you not won, you wouldn't have been created again somewhere down the line. Each and every single combination of sperm and egg would have resulted in somebody different (mention identical twins and I'll reach through the book and kick you) and the winner just so happened to be you. Congratulations! I've never been a fast runner, but at least at one moment in time, I was considered the best swimmer out of billions.

So you were a few-billion-to-one-chance-of-happening baby. That's already an awe-inspiring thing to imagine – but your parents were a few-billion-to-one-chance-of-happening babies, too. And so were their parents ... and *their* parents ... now, I'm not a mathematician, but imagine multiplying those probabilities throughout your ancestry. How are you here?! Again, you may put this down to fate, luck, coincidence or design – but none of those possibilities take away the fact that you being here as you are is mind-blowing. Not only do we have the multiplied odds to take into account over thousands of years, but let's look closer at your conception – not to be graphic (I'm sorry for this image), but what if your parents had decided not to try for you on that certain night? Or at that certain hour? At that certain second?! Would you still have won? Think about all the factors throughout the day of your conception that must have affected their decision to try for you. Think about all the factors that made it possible for your parents to meet, as far back as you can imagine, back to your great-great-great-great-great-great-grandparents. Every single conversation, every tiny little action, every single thought – the butterfly effect means that you were conceived not only by two people, but also by billions of events by millions of people over the course of thousands of years.

If you ever wonder whether life is worth fighting for, through all the pain and anguish – it took an awful lot of work to get you here. My great-great-great-great-grandfather didn't work to charm the pants off my great-great-great-great-grandmother for me to sit here and mope around. I'm sure if they'd lived long enough to understand the concept of memes, though, they'd be happy with my choice to sit around and watch them on a YouTube playlist until 2 a.m. instead of writing this book.

The Deadly Comparison

Comparing myself to others is something I have struggled with from the second I learned how to put two things side by side. Sadly, weighing up your own stats against someone else's – especially when you think highly of that person – can be lethal to your self-esteem. This goes for comparing looks, talent, wealth, material goods, relationship statuses and even emotional well-being. Comparison can very easily lead to a sense of jealousy, and becoming jealous or envious of a friend's accomplishments and lifestyle can destroy even the strongest of friendships – ultimately, nothing good comes from looking at someone else and saying, 'Why do they have that? Why don't I have that?'

Let me say something here: someone else's success does not correspond with your own. Becoming obsessed with being the best, smartest, richest or even most attractive person you know will make you lose sight of how good, smart, fortunate and attractive you already are. It actually wasn't until recently that

I heard a great phrase from my friend Lily: 'Comparison is the thief of joy.' Apparently it was Teddy Roosevelt who said that first, but I prefer to hold my friends in high enough regard that I convince myself they're just really profound. The saying is so, so true – as soon as you start comparing your own success and achievements to the success and achievements of somebody else, you are already lessening your own accomplishments and sense of pride, replacing them with bitterness and envy.

I'll use a personal example: Sure, one of my music videos that I worked really hard on reached over half a million views on YouTube, and that's incredible – but one of my friend's music videos got five MILLION in a shorter amount of time! Very quickly, without you even realising it, your brain will start to jump to other thoughts, such as, *Her music isn't even that good. Mine is better. Why did she get so many views, and I so few?* Immediately, you're pitting yourself against another person when you absolutely do not need to. It's even worse when the person you're juxtaposing with yourself is a friend. Whether you notice it immediately or not, you will begin to harbour a sense of resentment towards that person for daring to have/earn what you strive for. There are only a few things in life where competition means exclusivity – such as eating breakfast cereal. You only choose one cereal to eat, and don't go back to eat a bowl of a different type. Things such as songs, videos on YouTube and school grades are not limited edition. People won't just listen to one song, and then think, *Well, I've filled my quota for the day!* Nor will teachers think, *Well, I would give her an A, but I just gave out my one A grade for the day.* Someone else's success doesn't denote your failure.

Speaking of success – what is success to you? Is it fame? Is it money? Is it a statistic? Your own level of success should *always* and *only* be measured by your sense of happiness in how you're living your life. You do not have to be rich to be happy, nor do you have to have accolades, or be the head of a big organisation – you just have to make things that you're proud of, try your hardest to do the things you love, and spend time with the people you care about. Also – wanna hear a secret? We all compare ourselves to others, whether we like it or not, and others compare themselves to you all the time. Whether they're letting on or not, someone is fixated on something about you that they deem to be perfect. Feeling jealous/envious and comparing yourself to your peers or heroes is human nature – but it is vital that you overcome it and focus only on your own sense of success, and be happy for those you think are 'better' or 'more attractive' than you. Do not let your envy burn bridges – be happy for someone else's achievements, for they may not feel 'successful' at all, and keep walking down your own path, in your own shoes, for you can never walk in somebody else's.

As You See Others

Tell me, when you walk down the street and see a passer-by, how much do you notice about their appearance? As they approach you, do you stare at them, calculating what you consider to be their 'flaws'? Do you hone in on things such as their dress size or each individual spot on their face? Chances are (unless you're a very mean person) you don't. As soon as that person has walked past you, you've forgotten what they looked like, and you continue with your day.

That is what others do when they've seen you, too.

Struggling with your own self-esteem is a battle all of its own, but worrying about whether or not others perceive you as 'hot' or 'not' is futile. There was a YouTube trend a while back called *Smash or Pass* where YouTubers (mostly male) would bring up photos of other YouTubers (mostly female) and comment on whether they'd 'smash' or 'pass' them. On top of being grossed out by how objectifying this was, I mostly found myself in the 'pass' pile. A few years ago, I would have been devastated, but over the years, I have learned what I've been preaching throughout this book– a stranger's opinion on my appearance is irrelevant. *Oh, no! A YouTuber who treats women like trash wouldn't sleep with me! I'm so fucking sad about it!* Even if they'd said they'd 'smash' me, they wouldn't have the damn privilege.

There is a trick I taught myself which has really helped with pulling out the positives in my appearance when my mind is filled with self-doubt: whenever I do a meet and greet at events, I will look at the person approaching me and find something about their appearance I can compliment them on. Perhaps their hair looks super cute, or their make-up is totally on point, or their necklace is gorgeous! Over the course of a few years, I've taught myself to naturally find something positive to think and say about strangers I've never met before. I've gone from being someone who sees a person as entirely 'hot' or 'not' to appreciating the little features about everyone – and in doing so, I have also learned to do the same with myself. Now, when I look in the mirror, before my self-consciousness about my body or facial features can creep in, I remember the things I do like about myself. Sure, I've got permanent bags under my eyes (thanks, genetics) but my hair is growing longer each and every day, and looks healthy and strong! Sure, I don't have curves like the girls on Instagram that I love, but my tattoos on my arm are SUPER COOL. Sometimes, the only way out of a negative spiral is through fighting your own mind each and every day until you're able to see the things that others appreciate about you.

Let's do it together. Write down five things you like about yourself. It's okay if you have to think about it, but I will not accept 'I don't like anything about myself' as an answer. I bet your hair is cool. I bet your eyes light up super nice when you smile! I bet your butt looks great – wait, can I say that? Just pretend I said your nose is probably cute:

1.

2.

3.

4.

5.

When you're done, I want you to tweet me (@emmablackery) your answers. Let's celebrate your self-worth!

Don't you skip out on me! For every 'flaw' you think you have, there's something equally as cool about you that makes you unique. If you're really struggling, perhaps show this part of the book to your friends or a family member, and get them to tell you things they like about you. Agree with them. Don't try to downplay their compliments and brush them off! I know it can be hard accepting yourself for how you look, especially when there's so many hot pieces of ass out there (honestly why do I not look like Hayley Williams yet? I've been so good lately), but referring back to a list of things that you are comfortable with in terms of how you look can help to quieten those voices of self-doubt! I'll do it with you:

1. I have a nice smile! Sure, I had to get braces in adulthood to straighten my teeth out, but I'm super happy with them now, and I actually grin in photos instead of keeping my lips tightly shut!

2. My tattoos are TOTALLY RAD SICK COOL DOPE SHIBBY 360 NO SCOPE. Especially the ones on my right arm. I have a hamster wearing a kimono eating sushi permanently chilling out on my arm!

3. Sure, I'm short, but short is cute sometimes. It makes me appear younger, I never hit my head on doors and I'm always the last to get soaked in a rainstorm. Besides, anyone who doesn't take

me seriously because of my height is a proper bell who doesn't deserve to hang out with this short glass of water anyway.

4. My eyes are a nice shape! Every make-up artist tells me so. I don't know why make-up artists like to say it (perhaps they've all had bad experiences with . . . eyes that . . . aren't nice?) and when I smile my eyes light up and my entire appearance changes to that of a softer, kinder person. I can switch between a death glare and innocent, happy puppy eyes! I'm a master of disguise!

5. I have a cool birthmark on my hip that kind of resembles Switzerland. I just think it's neat.

Whenever I used to look in the mirror as a teenager, I would tug at the pores on my nose and pop every spot I had, praying that puberty would do me right. Now, when I stand in front of a mirror, I still get flashes of that unhappy, insecure teenager, but almost immediately, I see those five things on the positive list. It's taken a lot of years, a lot of anger directed at my body given to me by both my bullies and myself, but I've finally begun to focus on the things that truly matter: my family, friends, making music, experiencing new things, achieving my dreams, instead of worrying about the little lumps and bumps that get me down now and again.

11

Nourish Yourself!

You Are More Than Your Body

I've never been happy with my body. For as long as I can remember, I have wanted to change at least *one* thing about my appearance, whether it was the shape of my nose (not pointy enough) my jaw shape (too round, not enough neck) or my boobs (like two pain-killers on an ironing board, you know?). I'm not about to tell you that I've found a solution for insecurities, because I haven't. I still fight with my mind every time I see another woman I deem as 'perfect' or 'goals' in terms of appearance in magazines or on TV, no matter how much I tell myself they're either photoshopped or captured at a specific angle with good lighting on their side. In that very short, specific moment in time, it doesn't matter if their skin has been smoothed out, or if their waist has been digitally pinched in – they are perfect, and I am not.

However, I will say that, despite my ongoing insecurities, I have grown more comfortable with the genetics I was given. Over the past couple of years (which are, in my mind, the first years of my adulthood), I have come to the conclusion that my worth is not equal to my appearance. The happiness I feel from a compliment about my attractiveness is always fleeting, whereas the sense of accomplishment I feel within myself after creating something I am proud of (such as a 70,000-word book) stays with me for ever, my pride building and being deposited into a personal bank in my mind that I can withdraw from whenever I'm feeling down. *I have a spot on my upper lip? Who cares? I headlined Shepherd's Bush Empire on tour!*

If anything, the way I now react to someone calling me 'ugly' has completely flipped – when I was a teenager, battling with insatiable crushes and the monster that is puberty, my appearance meant everything to me. I wasn't confident in my abilities as a human, so I focused on trying to look attractive to make up for it. Whenever a kid walking past me in the corridor would call me an 'ugly goth bitch', I would brush it off, telling them and their friends where I would invite them to place their opinion (usually somewhere tight and dark that belonged to their mother). Then, when I was alone and away from their judging eyes, I would replay their insults in my mind, often bringing myself to the brink of tears. If those mean kids thought that about me, surely that meant that *everyone* thought that about me? It didn't matter how much of a smart, kind, funny person I tried to be – in my mind, I was *ugly*, and no one would take me seriously no matter how hard I tried.

Now whenever someone calls me ugly, I laugh at their cheap attempt to upset me. Oh, no! Someone I don't care about went for the go-to quick insult! Isn't *You're ugly* just the laziest insult in the world? Whether it's from a bully at school, or a comment online, I just cannot take it seriously anymore. When I first started to receive nasty comments, they really got underneath my skin, but after many years of receiving the same cruel messages every single day, I began to realise a few things. Firstly, attractiveness is subjective – really, they're stating an opinion, not fact – and secondly, if they're calling you 'ugly', they're not someone you want in your life, and therefore, their opinion means absolutely nothing! Now whenever I read *You're ugly*, or something else insulting my appearance, I'm able to translate it as *I do not find you sexually appealing to me*, and I breathe a sigh of relief, because, despite what I thought as an insecure young girl, that's not what I was put on the planet to be, and it's not something I would get fulfilment from. I wouldn't want someone so awful as to insult my appearance to find me attractive anyway.

Of course, that's just my personal growth. There will be people reading this who do get fulfilment from being considered attractive to others, and there is nothing wrong with that at all – I'm sure if you're a struggling model and you're called *ugly*, that word will sting you a little more than it would me – but the way to rebuild your confidence after an insult about your appearance is to focus on your self-worth. You always have the choice and freedom to bounce back after something hurtful, even if it takes a little while. You have the ability to deflect their attempts at upsetting you and turn them into a determination to do something that you're proud of, and whether you realise this at fifteen, twenty-five or forty-five, you will eventually be able to find that divide between a stranger's perception of you, and the perception you have of yourself. Achieve your goals in spite of the negative comments. Pity those who strive to hurt others with such cheap words, and know that you're a better person for not doing the same to them.

Of course, not caring about what others think and trying not to care about what *you* think are two very different things. There are still days when I'll look in the mirror and wish that my boobs were bigger, or my legs were stronger, or my tummy were flatter, and then feel this wave of shame that I'm not like the picture-perfect models or athletes who always look flawless. But here's my point, and I want you all to etch it into your brain: *I am more than my body.* My brain is more valuable than the sum of my visible parts. My pride in my abilities to create and love and *be loved* is stronger than any pride I would have in my would-be perfect appearance.

With this, I often remind myself of something I once said in a video many years ago: Think of your body as a vehicle. Your body, when it comes down to the wire, is a lump of carbon atoms all formed in a certain way to help transport you to your next destination. Your body will carry you to your friends, your family, your hobbies, your passions and to anything else that makes you happy. It gets you from A to B. You don't need a Porsche to get you from A to B – any car will do, whether it's a bit slow, or a bit rusty (this is a metaphor – if your body has signs of rust, please seek medical advice). Your 'vehicle' will get you where you need to go. It's like that cheesy thing your parents always say: it's what's inside that counts. Your body is simply a car to use to transport your soul to somewhere you love – respect it for that! Love your body for being able to make your soul happy – whether you think it's a sports car or a heap of junk. I'm not saying it's always going to be easy, but day by day, as your body carries you through experiences that an attractive appearance cannot help you with, you will slowly learn to accept yourself for who you are: warts and all.

Getting Out What You Put In

I'm not a nutritionist, and I'm not going to claim to be such a thing. I cannot sit here and write about macronutrients, or amino acid profiles – I don't have the nerve to do so. I don't believe that anyone untrained should be giving out advice when it comes to what you eat – every body is different, and needs different amounts of different things. However, I'm someone who's struggled with my own physical impairments, and have found that the way I fuel my body has had a life-changing effect. I was diagnosed with chronic fatigue syndrome at the age of seventeen, after contracting glandular fever and being given antibiotics that I later discovered I was allergic to. Whilst my case of CFS is mild, this syndrome often causes me to feel exhausted, no matter how much sleep I get, or how much of a routine I create for myself. I have struggled with my energy levels for almost ten years, and have only recently discovered the importance of eating well and truly nourishing my body. As I said in the section above, your body is your car. You can't expect it to function normally with no gas in the tank! By doing a lot of research and through trial and error, I came to discover the types of foods that my body needs in order to be at its best, and I hope that these simple nutrition 'hacks' can help you, too:

❧ Don't avoid fats! Don't believe the myth that fats make you fat. Of course, there's a difference between saturated, unsaturated and trans fats, but these things in moderation are perfectly healthy so long as they're part of a balanced diet. Healthy fats support cell growth, whereas unhealthy fats . . . well, once in a while, that junk food just makes you happy. Nothing wrong with that.

❧ Green food is the best food! If it's green, eat it (unless it's mould or something. Don't eat that). Find a vegetable you really love (or if you're a bit picky, find one you can tolerate) and smash that in wherever you can! My go-to vegetable is broccoli, which is packed full of nutrients and fibre. Try and make at least one third of the food on your plate the colour green. Add spinach, spirulina or kale to a smoothie! Eat avocados. Green foods will help with digestion and energy levels!

❧ Eat fruit! I used to try and avoid fruit because of the big fat sin: sugar. We're often told in news reports and on television shows that sugar is addictive, damaging and one of the worst things for us – but like fats, if you eat sugar in moderation and as part of a balanced diet, you're fine. In fact, switching out sweets for a banana or some strawberries is definitely advisable!

Sugary foods are definitely calorie-dense, but fruits, whilst high in fructose, contain so many vitamins, and are totally natural – so if you have a sweet tooth, don't be afraid of a fruit smoothie now and then! Carbs are *not* your enemy, they are your energy. Smash in the carbs before a long day of work, and you'll find yourself having more energy and focus throughout the day.

Speaking of calories – unless you are trying to gain muscle growth, you shouldn't be counting calories. Not even to lose weight. We often see calories as these tiny little devils that will rise up and make us 'fat' (and therefore 'undesirable', 'unattractive', 'of less worth') if we eat over 2,000 of them a day. Listen: so long as you're eating the right kinds of natural food, only eating junk food in moderation, staying hydrated and doing a fair amount of exercise, your body will have more energy, and will eventually work itself into the prime 'shape' for the amount of exercise it needs to do to get through the day. Calories, at their core, are simply units of energy – if you put in a lot of calories, you're putting a lot of energy into your body. If you allow that energy to build up, sure, it'll get stored as fat for later usage, but if you burn off energy as you go, you're going to be fine.

Stop counting calories, get your blood pumping and feel the difference very quickly!

- Breakfast is important. I know – I'm tired in the mornings, too. Who wants to get up early to eat porridge when you could just have another half an hour in bed? Fact is, breakfast fuels you right through until lunchtime, meaning you'll feel less sluggish and will be more alert than you would had you not eaten it. It also means you won't be tempted to snack on unhealthy things before lunchtime. You'll be surprised at how quickly your body will adjust to eating breakfast if you push yourself into a routine every morning.

The Simplest Trick

Ready for the biggest health hack of all? One that will improve your concentration and energy levels? One that will help viruses leave your body quicker? One that will help to lower inflammation? Here you go: Drink water. Lots of water. That's it!

Whilst I'm not stating that water is all you need when it comes to improving your health, being hydrated is by far the simplest action you can take to improving your energy levels, cognitive function and general health. For many years I was so dehydrated – my body simply got used to not drinking much, and thus, I never really got thirsty. Up until the age of twenty-four, I can recall only peeing twice a day – once in the morning, and once before bed. My pee was a dark, cloudy yellow (I cannot believe I'm talking about the colour of my pee in this book). I was constantly drained (having CFS didn't help, of course, but the difference between then and now is like night and day) and I lacked the ability to focus on any one task; I was snappy and rude to people and just generally felt *off* a lot of the time. Dehydration is a lot more serious and damaging to your health than you may realise – it can make you more susceptible to illness and exacerbate problems you already have.

It wasn't until October 2015 that I discovered the damage my unintentional dehydration was doing to my body. Because I wasn't regularly 'flushing the pipes', so to speak, I often contracted UTIs (urinary tract infections – they're surprisingly common, and don't imply anything about your hygiene or amount of sexual activity), and whilst they're easy to clear up with antibiotics, if you don't keep hydrated and clear out your system, they'll keep recurring – or, as in my case, get worse.

By the time I realised I had yet another UTI, it was too late. Within a few days of the initial symptoms, I had developed a persistent dull ache in my lower back, as well as just feeling generally unwell. I put it down to sleeping in a weird position and being a bit overworked – little did I know, the infection had spread to my kidneys. A few days later, my dad came to visit and only took one look at me before bundling me into his car and driving me to hospital. My skin had turned grey and I was barely able to concentrate on anything he was saying. When the doctors examined me, prodding me with every instrument they had (sounds more fun than it was), and taking enough blood to make me throw up and almost pass out, they discovered I had a severe infection that was making its way around my system. I had been extremely lucky that it had been caught when it had. If I had slept on my infection for one more day, the doctors told me, it most likely would have spread to my blood, and sepsis can become extremely difficult to treat. I was kept in hospital for four days, attached to a drip and bored out of my mind. The doctor who looked after me was shocked when I told her how little I drank – and after just one night on a drip, my skin was no longer grey. I was properly hydrated for the first time in years!

Ever since that stint in hospital, I have made sure I drink water at every opportunity – and now I'm able to detect when I'm even the slightest bit thirsty. I haven't had any infections since. I'm able to think more clearly, am more alert and less distracted – and if having to pee a few more times during the day is the only downside, I'll take it. Heed my warning! Your body needs water to function – if you like caffeinated drinks, be sure to drink ordinary water, too. Fizzy drinks and beverages such as coffee can actually make you feel worse after the initial caffeine buzz – water is the purest source of energy to keep your cells fuelled, even if it is a little boring. Your skin will be clearer, your weight more stable (you'll notice less water retention because your body no longer has to hold on to the little water it *does* get!) and you'll be in a better state of mind.

Man, I drank a lot of water writing this section.

The F-Word

Do you ever see those books on sale with a slender, blonde woman in workout gear on the cover, smiling like she actually bloody means it as she stands under the words, *How to transform your life through exercise!* and just think, Oh, fuck off? Sorry! I can't do it. I can't sit here and write about how exercise changed my life. I can't give you a before and after photo where I look like a blimp on the left and tanned, toned and *totally rejuvenated* on the right. I'm not here to insult those authors, or say that their methods don't work, but when I decided to write about fitness and exercise, I knew I'd have to be honest.

I bloody hate exercise with a passion. Unlike seemingly *everyone else* in the world, I don't get those endorphins that supposedly make you feel great after a workout. I cannot think of many things worse than waking up early to go to the gym – and believe me, I've tried. Getting out of bed at 6 a.m. in the freezing cold and doing exercise, or having a lie-in until 10 a.m. under the soft, warm covers of my bed? Tough choice!

However – I understand the repercussions of writing a book for young people in which I tell them not to bother exercising. Exercise *is* important – we all have an increasingly sedentary lifestyle. I sit at my desk writing, filming and editing most of the day, every day. I've sometimes looked down at the pedometer on my watch in the evening and seen that I've walked 200 steps – all day. If anything, it's quite a feat to be able to *only* walk 200 steps a day, but this isn't the time or place to joke about little victories.

Unfortunately for my fellow fitness-haters, exercise has too many benefits for us not to do it. It keeps our metabolisms in

check, it makes us more alert, it helps to prevent illness, it builds
stamina and strength should we ever need it (ever tried to lug a
flat-pack wardrobe up a flight of stairs? You need to be fit, and
also slightly mad). We cannot keep saying to ourselves, *Yeah, I'll
get fit eventually.* Start taking little steps towards becoming more
active. You don't need to be at the stage of a marathon runner to
enjoy the long-term benefits of light exercise. Here are some tips
that I've learned along the way to subtly increase your fitness level
without feeling exhausted and fed up with exercise altogether:

> ⚡ Do yoga! There are many free online tutorials
> and yoga sessions to try out that will help with
> your flexibility and muscle toning. When I'm not
> flat-out with work (such as, you know, writing
> 70,000 words) I exercise with DDP Yoga, which
> is hosted by a retired wrestler. It uses dynamic
> resistance, so you work against your own
> body without having to buy tons of expensive
> equipment, and your heart will be pounding
> without you doing any form of high-intensity
> cardio! I promise I wasn't paid to write that –
> it's just that good. If you'd rather practise more
> laid-back, relaxing exercise, then don't dismiss
> the benefits of stretching out your spine with a
> less intense form of yoga. Learning to take in
> oxygen at the right times can really help to clear
> your mind as well as get blood pumping around

your body. The best part? You can do it from the comfort of your own home! I personally can't stomach the idea of doing exercise classes with strangers (they're not looking at me – I know they're not – but it always feels like it). Yoga really only requires a mat and possibly some balance blocks (but they're not a necessity) and about half an hour a day. You might not notice the benefits immediately, but stick with it, do it once a day for a couple of weeks, and you'll begin to feel your body being less reluctant to move with you.

Travel to new places. I'm not saying take an exotic week out in Asia, or go and climb a mountain – a simple walk down unexplored streets will do the trick. If you live in a village and there's a street you've never needed to walk down, go and explore it (in broad daylight, of course. Make sure you feel safe at all times!). If you live in a built-up city, there's always a new street or a store you haven't been to! Go to that park you always walk or drive past. Sometimes, I get dressed, go outside and just walk. I just keep walking. I often get lost – thank goodness for GPS on phones these days – and sometimes, being lost is just what the body needs. When I was still living at home with my dad, I once went out on a walk

past my first primary school and stumbled upon
a massive field that I had no idea was there. It was
shrouded by bushes and trees, and was impossible
to see from the outside when walking past on
the street – it was only through pushing a bush
to one side that I was able to discover it. I ended
up visiting this large-but-secret field many times
throughout that summer. I'd lived around the
area for twenty years and had never seen it! It was
my secret place, where I could walk, listening to
my favourite music. As a stressed, overworked,
underpaid waitress, visiting that field kept me
sane that summer. Walking (especially to music,
in my case) is not only great and *vastly underrated*
exercise, but it also helps to clear your mind.
When you're not forcing yourself to sit in front of
a screen, your mind is no longer distracted by all
the things popping up in front of you, and you'll
find yourself able to think about things that are
troubling you in more depth and from a new
perspective.

For every hour you're sitting down – whether
it's at a desk or watching TV – stand up and
walk around for five minutes, or longer if you
can! It can be so easy to lose track of time when
you're working or watching a top-notch anime

(Shokugeki no Soma is my *shit*), but purposefully standing up and walking around will help stretch out your muscles and get blood flowing. I also find that when I'm sitting down, my body often falls into a state of tiredness and I find myself more prone to napping, which wastes time I could be using productively. Once you notice yourself in this seated position for too long (set a timer on your phone for fifty minutes if you find it hard at first), stand up and walk around. Go out and get some fresh air! If you find yourself fortunate enough to be able to do this more often than five minutes in every hour, then do! You'll find that you get more done by walking away from your desk for a few minutes than you do when you're distracted for hours sitting down.

Of course, I should probably add some buzz words: join a gym! Join a class! Go cycling with friends! Go for a jog! The truth is, I've tried all of these things, and not one of them has changed my life, because that's not what my body wants to do. Perhaps one day I'll do a workout at the gym and have an epiphany that exercise opens my mind, but for now, the little steps I can take, mixed with a healthy, balanced diet that includes a lot of protein and leafy greens, have helped me tremendously.

Oh, and also don't get caught up in the hype of fitness. It can be very easy to become addicted to exercise if you do feel an endorphin rush. If you find yourself feeling angry and wound up from *not* exercising, this is a sign that your brain is becoming dependent on fitness, and this can lead to an emotional dependency on eating right, which can be a slippery slope towards an eating disorder. Certainly reduce unhealthy foods, and do light exercise, but don't cut out your favourite foods entirely. Don't punish yourself for not exercising by skipping a meal. Schedule light workouts for, say, three times a week if you're trying to maintain a fitness level instead of training for marathons. Everything should be in moderation – and that includes the things that benefit you. If you feel as though you may be becoming emotionally dependent on exercise or you're deliberately trying not to consume enough calories, there are helplines at the back of this book that you can call for advice.

For clarity, I've been eating chocolate all the way through this section. Everything in moderation! That reminds me. I need to go and walk around for a while . . .

12

A Life Worth Living

The Life List

I make a lot of lists. I have to-do lists for the short-term, an ongoing list of video ideas, a list of people who I would totally *smash* (humans are flawed hypocrites, who knew?) and, most important of all, *the life list*. This is a list that I believe everyone on Earth should have, for numerous reasons. It is the list of things you wish to achieve in your lifetime, including the places you wish to visit and the things you'd like to own. I first created my initial *life list* out of boredom when I was twenty years old, having just started making YouTube videos. It was short, but it was filled with the goals I had made for myself:

- I want to be able to live on my own.

- I want to be able to do YouTube as a full-time job.

- I want to reach 100,000 subscribers.

- I want to travel to America.

- I want to buy a house.

- I want to get married and have children.

Slowly, as things were crossed off, such as quitting my waitressing job and reaching 100,000 subscribers, new goals were added. My goal of travelling to America transformed into wanting to visit all fifty states, and music goals such as 'release a debut album' were added. Currently, this is where I'm at with my life list:

- Buy a house and pay off the mortgage.

- Visit all fifty states of America.

- Visit Canada.

- Visit Japan.

- Visit Australia.

- Raise a total of £100,000 for Liberty in North Korea.

- Release a debut album.

- Release a song that has global recognition.

- Reach 2,000,000 subscribers on YouTube.

- Work in partnership with WWE.

- Own either a café or a fashion line.

- Get married and have children.

- Get a dog.

- ~~Write a book.~~

A life list is important to me for a couple of personal reasons. For one, it keeps me focused on the next step towards crossing off a goal. Being able to see your long-term or short-term goal in front of you as a physical statement, demanding to be achieved, helps encourage you to work hard for it. Once a goal is written down, you can no longer push it to the back of your mind, with the thought, *Yeah, well,* maybe *I'll do that, if I feel like it in the future.* It is there, waiting to be fulfilled. Of course, it's important to note that, if your focus shifts, it is completely okay to take something off your list. You should only write down things that you are passionate about achieving. For instance, whilst I would like to own a café in the future, I have a lot I want to achieve *before* starting on that, and somewhere along the way, perhaps it won't be something I am passionate about achieving any more. If that time comes, I'll cross it off – I'm sure it'll have been replaced by something else that has captured my passion and attention. Also, it's important to note that whilst these are long-term goals, I still celebrate the short-term goals that help me get to where I want to be. It's all about the little pictures, remember?

Second of all, the list serves as a means to remind me of how much there is to experience in the world. There are 195 countries in the world that I can choose to put on that list to visit, and the sense of accomplishment I feel when I achieve a goal that relates to the things I love, such as YouTube and music, is worth sticking around for. If you are someone who is perhaps feeling complacent with the world, and wondering if your life has any purpose, *give* it purpose. The world, despite its flaws, is a ginormous, beautiful place, filled with some wonderful humans and breathtaking sights. Start your *life list* with places you wish to visit, whether it's Machu Picchu or Tiananmen Square, and start working towards finding ways to make those dreams happen! Slowly work up towards expanding your list to career goals and things to do with your passions, as you discover them. Your *life list* should serve as a reminder of all the possibilities you have on this planet, despite its occasional awfulness. The sense of accomplishment is a thousand times stronger than the feeling of hopelessness.

What is on your *life list*?

Looking Ahead (And Looking In Front Of You)

When I was younger, my main emotion was worry. Whilst I would still classify myself as a bit of a *worrier*, I am no longer led by my fear of bad things happening. As I mentioned previously, I've struggled a lot with *catastrophic thinking* – essentially, fearing the worst. I was convinced that I was going to fail my GCSEs, and therefore not get into college. Not getting into college meant not being able to get a degree, and *that* meant never having a well-paid job. No one would want to fall in love with someone in a dead-end job, so I would be alone for ever. I managed to map out my entire future as a failure before I'd even truly begun to start living. To me, at the age of fifteen, if I didn't get the highest grades imaginable, my life was *over*. I wasn't enrolled in a stage school as a young child, and my voice wasn't the strongest in the world – so I would never be a successful musician. I spent my time waitressing consumed with the fear of being fired and never being able to find another job. I was so fixated on looking ahead that I became spiritually short-sighted. I was so stuck on fearing the worst that I set aside no time to simply relax and enjoy being young. This, coupled with my anxiety issues, meant that my teenage years were (in my opinion) completely wasted. I spent my early youth acting like an elderly woman – always trying to make the right impression, led by fear instead of love.

I am not going to sit here and be all clichéd and say something like *don't worry about anything! Life is too short! YOLO!* The truth is: a little bit of worrying is healthy. It means that you *care*. However – it is important not to let your life be led by negative feelings. I do not always 'live in the moment' – I often have to plan far ahead with music releases and video ideas – but whenever I can, I try my hardest now to simply live my life day by day. Sometimes, when I'm really lucky, I can plan my life from one meal to the next. I prioritise my happiness and social life over things that will stress me out (even if it does mean having to work a little harder to catch up sometimes!). I see my family as often as I can, I go shopping with friends, and most of all, I don't take things as seriously as I used to. I know that there will be times when you won't feel as though you can take time out from your schedule to just relax, but I can guarantee there will be a few moments a week when you could definitely be kinder to yourself – always take those opportunities.

An overwhelming majority of the time, I'm able to see insults and gossip about me online as just words on a glowing screen. That glowing screen doesn't even have to glow at all if I choose not to let it. I can uninstall social media apps from my phone (I often do) and enjoy living in a world away from the Internet every now and again. I go for walks listening to my favourite music. I see my friends without feeling the need to post about it online (because if you hang out with friends and don't take a group selfie to prove it, did you really hang out with them at all?). If I begin to feel fear about a deadline, I try to schedule a light, even amount of work towards that deadline over a few days, and then treat myself if I do the amount of work I'd pledged to do. If I feel a personal issue with friends or family begin to escalate, I will do my best to solve it as soon as possible without bottling my feelings up. If an issue doesn't concern me, I will no longer get involved like I used to, but simply mind my own business. Over the past year of my life, I have made a lot more time for myself, despite being busier than ever – and my mental health, whilst still fragile at times, is doing much better overall.

As I said in Chapter Two about my experience with anxiety, as much as we like to worry about little things in life, ultimately, *worrying does nothing.* Worrying about a problem, as opposed to actually taking steps to solve it, is counter-productive. It will add stress and make you prone to exacerbating the situation. Worrying has zero benefit to your well-being. Of course, not worrying is easier said than done, but I am a testament to the correlation between getting older and caring less. Over time, you'll find yourself becoming hardened to things that you've come across before, and you'll find yourself *far too tired* to deal with stress that doesn't need to be at the forefront of your mind. Over the past couple of years, I've honestly found that I've started to care less about what people think of me, without making a conscious effort. Once you stop allowing fear and worry to rule your life, you will no longer be in the passenger seat of your own existence: you will be driving, cruising at whatever speed you like, taking the scenic route whenever you choose, with your favourite music blaring through the speakers. This may seem a world away to you right now – but my journey to happiness has been long and arduous. I'm not even at my final destination yet, but I'm going forwards, not backwards, and in time, if you're not already – you will too.

Life Is Not A Movie

The problem with living in a society obsessed with celebrity culture and the entertainment industry is that we grow up alongside television and movies as much as we do our parents.

The first movie I remember falling in love with was *Toy Story*, which came out when I was four years old. As well as becoming convinced that sentient toys would become active as soon as my back was turned (I would spend hours trying to 'sneak up' on my toys, but those fuckers are *quick*, let me tell you), I also began to believe the narrative of *things always work out. There is always a happy ending.*

It isn't really until your early teens that you begin to understand that sometimes that isn't the case. The guy doesn't always fall in love with the girl. The hard-working student doesn't always get the highest grades and get accepted into their chosen university. Parents do not always get back together. Friendships are not always mended after a massive fall-out. Truly, along with hormones, learning the hard lesson that life is *not like the movies* comes as a huge shock to the system, and it is often overlooked as a reason for so many cases of depression in teenagers. Adults (or at least people my age and above) reading this might be scoffing, thinking, *Well, kids have to learn! They need to stop expecting everything to fall into their laps and grow up!* But deep down inside, that *happy ending* narrative stays with us all. In a world where we are told by the media and really clichéd hipster posters to keep up the 'good vibes', we all desperately wish for the problems in our lives to be solved quickly, effortlessly and painlessly.

In the real world, shit happens. All of the time. We don't get a callback after a job interview. Our relatives die. Our relationships break down. Our mental health takes a beating. A typical movie will follow the traditional plot points: protagonist is introduced, progress is made, protagonist faces a conflict/dilemma, all hope is suddenly lost, a cheesy pep talk happens, action is taken, the conflict/dilemma is solved, everyone is happy. Life simply isn't like that. We will face hardships at random intervals, and they're not always followed by pep talks and a heroic comeback. The sooner you stop treating life as one big search for a happy ending and accept that life is a constant wave of trials and tribulations, solving each and every little problem as it comes instead of worrying about the big picture – your life will improve.

Say that you've always had the dream of getting married. Despite your job aspirations and hobbies and passions, the thing you want more than anything is to walk down the aisle. You meet the person of your dreams, get engaged, and finally the big day arrives. Everything is perfect and goes without a hitch. If your life were a movie, it would stop at a freeze-frame as you drive off into the sunset in your car that has *JUST MARRIED* sprayed on the back window.

Your life does not end the second you achieve your dream of being wed. Instead, your dreams change with you. Now, the challenge is to find a new goal that consumes your being and drives your existence, as well as maintaining a healthy marriage. You were so fixated on your one goal of getting married that anything after your wedding was unprepared for. Let's change it slightly: say that your dream has always been to become a vet. You go to college, you go to university, you get the qualifications you need, and finally, you're hired. You're doing the job you've dreamed of having since you were a child. The end! Roll credits. Only, your job, whilst being something that you love, will often be challenging – you will have great days, and you will have terrible days. Either way, your heart will continue beating, and you hadn't really thought about what you wanted for your life past the point of being hired to stick a thermometer up a cat's butt (I'm sorry, vets – I've never had to use your services, so in my mind, this is all I envision you do on a day-to-day basis. People also think I just talk to a camera five minutes a week, so trust me when I say I mean no disrespect to your craft).

The trick is not to have a definite end goal in life, which is hard when that is all you're pressured into conjuring up for yourself when you're going through school. From the moment we're old enough to understand pictures on flash cards, our parents are asking us what we want to *be* when we're older, as if a career is the most vital thing in our existence as opposed to good health, happiness and a sense of freedom. Sadly, it is money that makes the world turn, not love and kindness, and this is why we are taught from colostrum (don't look that word up) to value money and strive to get a well-paid job in order to be *happy*. Of course, a well-paid job is great – a job you love is even better – but material accomplishments should be goals along the way, not at the end of the rainbow. Instead, our long-term goals should be emotional ones, such as feeling happy and proud of ourselves, experiencing love and making memories with our friends and family, seeing the world and experiencing the joy that freedom brings to the soul. Once you learn the difference between the initial feeling of satisfaction you get from acquiring something new and the long-term feeling of being in a good mental state, your life will improve. You will begin to prioritise the things that make you truly happy. You will say yes to more exciting prospects, and no to the more tedious ones. You will open yourself up to loving, and being loved, and when your credits do finally roll, not at the end of an achievement, but at the end of a long, happy life, I hope you'll be proud of the unique, non-formulaic movie you directed.

I know, I said life *wasn't* a movie, all right? Don't get technical on me. It was a cool sentence to end the chapter on, and now we've ruined it. I suppose I could just delete that last sentence. Oh, and the one I just wrote. You know what? It's like I said – not everything has a perfect ending. It's not the destination that counts, but the journey, right? Let's move on before I start saying 'YOLO' un-ironically.

13

The Tough Son of a Gun

The New You

At the very start of this book, the end of which we are nearing, I said, 'This book won't change your life.' I never set out to write a book that would revolutionise your way of thinking – only to document my own journey from being a weak, depressed teen to becoming the stronger, happier person that I am today, stating what I would do differently now as though I were having a conversation with my former self. If my words have helped you in any way so far, that is the best bonus I could've hoped for. In this final chapter, I want to talk about a few changes I have been able to make to my attitude towards life that have transformed the way I live. I am, by all accounts, a stubborn, persistent motherfucker of a woman, a far cry from the weak-willed doormat of a girl I was just ten years ago. It has taken a lot of time and a lot of lessons learned the hard way in order to develop the self-confidence and assertiveness I own today, and I have no doubt that, just like they were for me, these words of advice will be hard to follow immediately. In fact, I am willing to bet that these lessons will be of little use to you until you naturally discover them for yourself. However – I am going to give them to you regardless. Do with them what you will:

Learn the power in saying no. By this, I don't mean going out of your way to cut someone down to size, or make them feel insignificant. Growing up, as I've said, I was a doormat. I was susceptible to peer pressure, despite being adamant that I was strong-willed; I would do anything my friends told me to do out of desperation to keep them around; I quit my job in the shoe shop because I felt intimidated; I would work unpaid overtime whenever I was asked because I was afraid of losing my job. Over time, you will lose patience for doing things that do not benefit you. Let me tell you: you do *not* have to look after your friend's sister's incontinent dogs just because someone asked you nicely, and if your 'friend' is the type of person who would think badly of you for unashamedly saying that you don't have time or that you simply don't want to, they're a shitty 'friend'. Of course, I am not saying you shouldn't do favours for friends – kindness makes the world a better place, and one day, that favour will (or at least should) be repaid in kind – but there will come a time when you reach a pivotal moment with your sanity when you realise that you *have* to start becoming more selfish. Be kind where you can, but most importantly, make time for yourself; treat yourself as though you are your own best friend. Say no to things that will upset you or distract you from your own projects when you can't spare the time. If you don't feel like going out clubbing with friends, you don't have to go if you truly don't want to. You will begin to thank yourself when you focus on your own happiness after being selfless for so long.

You also do not have to justify why you are saying no to something – the word 'no' is enough. You do not have to be rude when declining to go somewhere or do someone a favour, but also you do not owe anybody an explanation. If you don't want to do something you don't have to, and that is enough of a reason to give. If your friend is asking you in that *really annoying tone*, 'Ohhh, come on, it'll be fun! Why not?' you do not have to give a bogus reason or excuse. Simply state, 'I just don't feel up to it. I'll make it up to you another time. Have a great night.'

You do not need to live in fear of your bosses at work either, so long as you are adhering to your contract and job description. Management – particularly in large companies and franchises – is there to protect you. You cannot be forced to work more hours than you are contracted to, and you cannot expect to be reprimanded for not going above and beyond without being paid for your time. You cannot be fired for requesting a holiday that is entirely within your contractual rights.

Once you stop allowing the people in your life to walk all over you, and stop trying to justify why you are saying no, you will become more confident and truly begin to feel in control of your time and emotions. I encourage you still to seize new opportunities, and to see friends you care about whenever possible, but if you feel as though someone is taking advantage of you or trying to force you into doing something you don't actually have to do, you have every right to kindly say the word 'no'. Take the word we were raised to associate with negativity and flip it on its head – saying 'no' can be a very positive thing for your own well-being.

Stand up for yourself. This definitely ties in with the last point about being able to confidently say no, but everything you want to be is on the other side of your fear. If you are being teased or bullied, don't let it slide. Take the necessary steps in order to make it stop. If someone you consider a friend is allegedly gossiping about you behind your back, confront them and ask them if the rumours about their gossiping are true. Cut out anyone who makes you feel inferior and who refuses to change their ways. If you recognise a relationship is turning toxic, seek help if necessary, and leave. Life is *far* too short to be lived as a meek, downtrodden shell of a human. Have confidence in your capabilities, and try to see yourself as you see your heroes: strong, empowered, confident, the opposite of worthless. If someone is upsetting you, don't take it lying down. Do not let someone else – whether they are close to you or not – make you feel small, weak or stupid. Do not allow yourself to remain in scenarios where you are suffering. Stay strong, fight back, and stand up for yourself at any given moment. What's the alternative?!

Get back up. We've spoken about this already – rejection is tough. Sometimes, someone you fancy (if you are unlucky enough to fancy anybody) won't reciprocate your feelings. That book you've worked hard on and submitted to tons of publishing companies might get rejected across the board. You might not get that call-back for that dream job that you've been sitting by the phone for. You might feel as though you've found your *forever boy/girl*, as I did, and then they might slip through your fingers. Whilst depression and feeling sad about a loss or rejection is not a choice, having your moment of emotions and then getting back up and out there in order to try again is a conscious effort that is always available to you. Some rejections will be harder than others to recover from – a bad break-up can make you feel unable to get back on the dating scene for years, and every rejection can feel like another chip at your block of self-confidence. It is okay to feel knocked down, but it is imperative that you get back up again, just like the Chumbawamba song says. You know the one. At the end of the day, when you have been knocked down, you have two choices – you can stay down, winded, wallowing in your injured pride and shame for days, weeks, months or even years, or you can slowly fight your way back on to your feet, with less pride but far more experience, having learned a valuable lesson about how to avoid getting knocked down in the same way again. Get knocked down, get back up again, and never let them keep you down.

Not everyone is going to like you. Get over it. Up until very recently, I was obsessed with the idea of getting my online critics to change their opinions of me. I feel as though this stemmed from working as a waitress where I got on with all my colleagues and filming videos for a small audience who truly all loved what I was making, to expanding and growing an audience from viral videos and word of mouth. As if out of nowhere, I suddenly had people I had never met being sceptical and/or critical of everything I did (even a few months in to writing this book I stumbled across a post about me, claiming that my book deal couldn't *possibly* have happened as I'd described in a video, and that I *had* to be lying about how long I'd been in talks with my publisher!). I became extremely insecure, just as I'd been as a teenager, second-guessing every line in my videos, every tweet or post, reading them over and over again until I was sure they wouldn't offend someone and start a site-wide backlash.

The fact is that no matter what you do – whether you're at school, work or you're an 'online personality' (or as the journalists like to call us, 'Internet sensations that make MILLIONS just sitting in their bedrooms') – there will be people who just don't like you, just as *you* don't like everyone you come across, either. Eventually you will find yourself at the receiving end of someone else's impressions and opinions. Whilst you can do everything in your power to try and convince these people that they are wrong about you, life becomes easier once you accept that these people who don't like you have already made up their minds about you. It sounds clichéd as all hell, but try your hardest to focus on the people who dedicate their time to caring about you and appreciating what you do, rather than wasting it on people who want to tear you down. If you only had ten minutes to live, and you had to choose between spending those ten minutes in a room filled with your loved ones or in a room filled with your haters, which would you choose? When the aspect of time comes into play, we all choose to accept love. Change your perspective – those who mind don't matter, and those that matter don't mind. You are most likely not going to change the minds of people who don't like you – at its very core, it's either jealousy, chemistry, or both. Hearing someone talk shit about you or socially reject you can really fucking sting, but in time, that pain will bounce right off your thick skin.

Now, when hearing about someone who doesn't enjoy my music or my video content, I respect it. Taste is subjective. I'm not about to go and confront them and ask, 'Well, why *don't* you like me? What did I do? What can I do to change that?' because I know I'll never get the answer I want without having to change the things I really like about myself. I'm going to let them call me 'annoying', or say that this book is a pile of dog shit, and I'm going to carry on creating – both for myself and for people who support me, such as yourself. You cannot turn your haters into your lovers – it is a futile exercise.

If you are being bullied or harassed, do what you need to in order to neutralise that situation, be it telling a teacher, parent or higher management at work, but turn that helplessness and desperation for approval into a strength, simply by choosing to draw a line under them and walking away with your head held high. It won't be easy at first, but your skin will thicken in time and with age. Someone doesn't like you? Big fucking deal! Who honestly cares, besides you? If you stop caring, then no one cares about their often irrational hatred! You take their power from under them in one fell swoop by flicking your *care switch* to Off. Remember that as with bullies, the amount of time that critics remain an important part of your life is entirely up to you. They won't stick around to talk about you for ever, but even if they persist, once you are able to train your brain to no longer give them much thought, it's as though they don't exist. This goes for strangers on the Internet, too. Block them or mute them, and cyber-walk away. Let them shout into the void whilst you drown them out with the sounds from the people who spend their time appreciating you for your weird, wacky self.

Your Eighty Years

I truly cannot believe we're here at the end. I've made it all the way through the writing process, and you've made it through all of my weird anecdotes and often nonsensical metaphors. I feel as though we've both achieved something here. If this book was a human, we'd now be looking at an old man – one who has lost a lot, but is still smiling. 'What other choice do I have?' he asks, chuckling to himself as he looks back at bittersweet memories of old, captured in photographs. With this . . . nonsensical metaphor, I want to talk about getting old. Like, *old* old.

On average, a typical human in the Western world will live to be approximately eighty years old. You may be thirteen, a sixth of the way through your life, or you might be twenty-five, a third of the way through. I'm not trying to give you a crisis – but when you reach the age of eighty, or surpass it, your time is limited. From this moment on, you have the rest of your eighty years to do as much as you've set out to do as possible. At best, you've been given around eighty years to explore the world, learn skills that interest you, climb career ladders, start a family (should you choose to), and then before you know it, it's over. Death, as you know by now, used to terrify me – not so much my own mortality, but that of my loved ones. I have had to make peace with the fact that death is inevitable, and in doing such, I have begun to regret how little I truly *lived* through my early years, and am trying my hardest to make up for it.

In 2012, when I was twenty-one years old, I filmed and uploaded a video called 'One Chance'. In it, I spoke about the importance of chasing a dream if you have one, as well as lamenting my lack of motivation in my teenage years. I speak about how, when I first discovered music with guitars, I would sing into a hairbrush, pretending I was performing on stage to a crowd who had bought tickets to see me, dreaming of being friends with my favourite band, Busted. Although I was only fourteen, and limited by my inability to attend a stage school, I look back at my wasted teenage years filled with regret for the after-school clubs I didn't fight to join, as well as the musician kids at school I could have tried to befriend and write music with. Instead, I was preoccupied with trying to be liked, by my peers and my crushes, barely picking up my neglected guitar that my dad had bought me and making him feel as though he had wasted his money.

Whilst I do not hold my blow with anxiety against myself (if I woke up every morning and blamed my mental health issues on myself, I wouldn't want to wake up, simple as that), I sometimes sit back and reflect on all the opportunities I couldn't bring myself to take: the teaching degree I never studied for, the lifelong friendships I would have made at university (as well as the sense of independence I would have gotten there), the holidays with friends and press events abroad that I bailed on . . .

Just as it does no good to worry, it does no good to reflect with regret. Those years, however wasted, are behind me now. I cannot get them back. I do not get a do-over. These were the cards I was dealt, and I have to keep playing my hand. All I can do is ensure that the remainder of my eighty years is spent in such a way that my early life pales in comparison. Whilst I am not the master of living life to the full, I am no longer afraid of taking opportunities to make wonderful memories. I say yes and no to the appropriate things; I travel the world whenever I'm able to; I make sure to visit my family and see friends often; I practise guitar and write songs whenever I feel inspired, and work hard to play the shows to the crowd that I dreamed of as a teenager.

Did I mention that Busted got back together and I got to tour with them? I'm fairly sure I mentioned that. It only took twelve years(!)

The bottom line is: you truly get one chance to nail this 'life' thing. There are no do-overs (at least, not in your current vessel, should you believe in reincarnation) and there will be times when you have hated entire days and haven't lived life to the fullest – that is okay. Rest days are super important! However – your clock is ticking. You have eighty years to live the best life you possibly can. You can spend those eighty years however you want – it's your life, after all. You can spend them dreaming, or you can spend them *doing*. You can spend them defeated, or you can spend them *fighting*. You can fill your brain's photo album to the brim with memories and gorgeous sights, or you can choose to leave it blank. Ultimately, at the end of it all, when you and I are approaching the end of our short time here, we'll be saying one of two things:

'I'm glad I tried that.'

'I wish I'd tried that.'

I cannot personally think of a scenario more depressing than being an elderly lady on my deathbed, with nothing but my memories to reflect on, and finding that there aren't as many as I'd hoped. I dread the thought of being in a hospital and remembering times when I backed out of doing something, and wishing with all my might I had the power to go back and do it. Regret is one of the most dull-ache emotions you can experience, and so it is up to you to minimise that final pang of regret you will feel when it is too late to do something about it. As I said earlier – everything you want in life is on the other side of your fear. Talk to those intimidating cool kids that you want to be friends with. Tell your crush that they're cute. Climb that career ladder. Take that day off. Go on that holiday. Put in that time towards your passion. Write that song. Write that book. Take that chance. If it all goes tits-up, well, that's gonna suck for some time, but at least, when you're able to dust yourself off and get back up, you'll be proud of yourself for having tried. It will always be better to say 'I wish I hadn't done that' than 'I wish I'd tried that'.

My final plea to you, after you've stuck around reading my words for so long, is this: if there is something that you dream of doing (that is legal, obviously) then *please* do everything in your power to do it. Chase after it. Make mistakes and learn from them. Don't waste your limited time on this planet because you're sitting in the passenger seat next to your fear. Don't spend your time worrying about your critics. Don't waste your life trying to impress the people who don't like you for who you are. Do whatever you need to do to be in that deathbed, smiling, saying, 'Man . . . I had a good run.'

After twenty-five years of tears, mistakes, anguish, fear, anxiety, depression and regrets – and then love, friendship, memories, sightseeing, laughter, accomplishing dreams and slowly discovering who I truly am . . . yeah, I'm happy here. I feel good. I leave you with my favourite quote:

> 'Stay hungry, stay foolish.'
>
> – Steve Jobs

I hope you feel good, too.

Emma ♥ x

Resources

If you're reading this section and considering reaching out to these services for help – I want to offer you the biggest congratulations! It truly takes a lot of guts not only to admit that you are struggling, but also to choose to take action and do something about your problems. I've spent many years being too afraid to seek help. *What if they think I'm being stupid? What if they tell me that I'm making things up?* I also still find myself with an irrational fear of talking to strangers on the phone to the point where calling for a taxi is an arduous task – so don't worry, you're not alone.

With that said, I feel as though before I leave you, I must state this: You're not being stupid. The services listed below employ trained professionals, who will have listened to many others with similar issues more times than you can imagine:

UK

- SAMARITANS – free confidential support for anyone in distress.
  www.samaritans.org / 116 123 (Freephone helpline, 24 hours a day, every day.)

- NHS – find advice regarding medical treatment.
  www.nhs.uk
  Call 111 for any non-emergency medical assistance (Freephone, 24 hours a day, every day.)
  Call 999 for emergencies only.

- CHILDLINE – free confidential advice for children and young people.
  www.childline.org / 0800 1111 (Freephone helpline, 24 hours a day, every day.)

- THE MIX – a support service and online resource for young people, offering advice on a variety of issues.
  www.themix.org.uk / 0808 808 4994 (Freephone helpline, 11 a.m.–11 p.m. every day.)

- BROOK ADVISORY SERVICE – advice and support for anyone under 25 on sex, contraception, pregnancy, sexual health and abortion. Drop-in appointments available at clinics nationwide.
  www.brook.org.uk

- MIND – charity providing information and support on a range of mental health issues.
  www.mind.org.uk / 0300 123 3393 (Infoline, 9 a.m.–6 p.m., Monday to Friday. Calls charged at local rates.)

- SWITCHBOARD – helpline providing support and advice for LGBT+ people.
  www.switchboard.lgbt / 0300 330 0630 (10 a.m.–10 p.m. every day.)

Ireland

- SAMARITANS – free confidential support for anyone in distress.
  www.samaritans.org / 116 123 (Freephone helpline, 24 hours a day, every day.)

- CHILDLINE – free confidential advice for children and young people.
  www.childline.ie / 1 800 666 666 (Freephone helpline, 24 hours a day, every day.)

- SPUNOUT – a support service and online resource for young people, offering advice on a variety of issues.
  www.spunout.ie

- JIGSAW – organisation providing mental health support to people under 25.
  www.jigsaw.ie

- LGBT Helpline – confidential helpline for LGBT people in Ireland.
www.lgbt.ie / 1 890 929 539 (6.30 p.m.–9 p.m., Monday to Wednesday; 6.30 p.m.–10 p.m., Thursday; 4 p.m.–10 p.m., Friday; 4 p.m.–6 p.m., Saturday and Sunday)

Australia

- LIFELINE – free confidential support for anyone in distress.
www.lifeline.org.au / 13 11 14 (24 hours a day, every day.)

- KIDS HELPLINE – free confidential counselling service for anyone between the ages of five and twenty.
www.kidshelp.com.au / 1 800 55 1800 (24 hours a day, every day.)

- REACHOUT – a support service and online resource for young people, offering advice on a variety of issues.
www.au.reachout.com

- BEYONDBLUE – organisation providing information and support on mental health issues.
www.beyondblue.org.uk / 1 300 22 4636 (24 hours a day, every day.)

- For support and resources for LGBT+ people in Australia, visit:
www.healthdirect.gov.au/lgbti-mental-health

New Zealand

- SAMARITANS – free confidential support for anyone in distress.
  www.samaritans.org.nz / 0800 726 666 (Freephone help-line, 24 hours a day, every day.)

- YOUTHLINE – free confidential support and advice for young people.
  www.youthline.co.nz / 0800 376 633 (Freephone helpline, 24 hours a day, every day.)

- For information about mental health services in New Zealand, visit:
  www.mentalhealth.org.nz

- OUTLINE – free confidential support for LGBTQI+ people in New Zealand.
  www.outline.org.nz / 0800 688 5463

USA

- NATIONAL SUICIDE PREVENTION LIFELINE – free confidential support for anyone in distress.
  www.suicidepreventionlifeline.org / 1-800-273-8255 (Freephone helpline, 24 hours a day, every day)

- PLANNED PARENTHOOD – advice, support and health-care for women on sex, contraception, pregnancy, sexual health and abortion.

    www.plannedparenthood.org / 1-800-230-7256 for an appointment.

- THE TREVOR PROJECT – service offering crisis intervention and suicide prevention for young LGBTQ people aged 18–24. **www.thetrevorproject.org** / 1-866-488-7386 (24 hours a day, every day)

- NAMI (National Alliance on Mental Health) – organisation providing information and support on a range of mental health issues. **www.nami.org** / 1-800-950-6264 (10 a.m.–6 p.m. ET, Monday to Friday.)

In the *extremely* unlikely situation that you do not receive exceptional service from the places listed above, lodge a complaint and do not let it deter you from seeking treatment in order to be truly happy. Getting help does not make you stupid – it makes you brave.

    Take care of yourself. Go and have a wonderful life. If it hasn't already begun, then it begins today.

To The Ones I Love . . .

Whilst *Feel Good 101* took many long, exhausting hours to create, this book of life lessons has been twenty-five years in the making. So many people have entered my life and graced me with their love, knowledge and experiences that it would be near impossible to thank them all.

Firstly, I must start with the team at Little, Brown Book Group for being directly responsible for making *Feel Good 101* everything that I envisioned it to be, including Aimee Kitson, Clara Diaz and Nico Taylor. Their constant help and guidance has been nothing short of wonderful and has made writing this book a wonderful experience! A special thank you must go to Hannah Boursnell, the truest of all of the babes, who has worked tirelessly with me from the very conception of this book to make it what it is today. Thank you for putting up with my stubbornness, pleas to extend deadlines and awful jokes. This book would not exist without you, or at least, if it *did*, it would be right shit.

Thank you to my wonderful book agent, Richard Pike at Conville and Walsh, for always pushing to get the most from me, and for doing all of the things that my brain simply just does not have the capacity to do – on top of coping with sleepless nights with a newborn baby! You are an everyday hero.

Mark Walker – truly, I do not know where I would be without your support, love and guidance as my manager. You have to put up with *so much* of my shit. I'm short-tempered, always flip-flopping between ideas and always late – and you're still here, putting your faith in me each and every day and working until the early hours to make my life better. As well as being an incredible manager, you are one of my closest friends. Thank you for everything you do, from the bottom of my heart.

To my wonderful parents – I'm sorry for being a bit difficult through the teenage years. I hope I've made up for it all by now, and I aim to make you proud of me each and every day. To my mother Sheila, who always manages to tackle adversity and hardships with a smile on her face – despite all that we have been through together, I am so happy that we came out of the other side much closer and also much stronger. To my wonderful dad, Michael – my best friend in the entire world, and the human I look up to the most in the world – I have said this to you many times now, but if I ever manage to become just half of the strong, loving, dedicated, carefree person that you have always been towards me, then I will be happy. I am forever proud to be a Blackery. I love you both so much, and your unwavering love and support of every decision I have made (except the Madonna piercing, I guess) have made me into the person I am today. If you think I suck, well, that's well and truly on you.

To my sister Febe and my brother Travis – this book, as I write it, is filled with life lessons that you have yet to learn. Not everything in this book will make sense to you right now, but when you come across hardship, my stories will be here waiting for you, even if I am thousands of miles away. You are both such good kids – please don't ever lose your curiosity and optimistic outlook on life. Those two things will be essential in making you happy. I love you both so much, and I just know you will both grow up to make me incredibly proud – follow your heart at all costs, chase your dreams, and never give up, even when that's what people want you to do.

To my best friend Leesa, my partner-in-crime at school when I needed you the most – I was truly lost without you, and although we can't see each other as often as we'd like, I know that you are always there for me, and I hope you know that I am always going to be there for you, too. Thank you for fourteen years of stupid inside jokes and for having my back in the most stressful of situations. I didn't tell the story about the time I walked out of school and had the police called, did I . . .? Oh, well. I guess I'll just have to write another book and tell everyone how wonderful you truly are!

To Lily Melrose – our shared jokes are a little too explicit to put in this book. Thank you for truly teaching me what it means to not worry about the little things that don't matter. Before we became friends, I was a real worrywart, but you are helping to shape me into a happier, more carefree person each and every day. Thank you for sitting up until 4 a.m. with me every few weeks to watch wrestling live on TV, thanks for always coming out for bubble tea with me when I need to vent about something, and thanks for being my friend. You make me feel cool.

Carrie Hope Fletcher – not gonna lie, I'm putting you in my thank-yous simply because you didn't put me in *your* thank-yous for *All I Know Now* and I just wanted to make you feel bad. I'm kidding (sort of) – you know very well that it was your advice book back in 2015 that made me realise that writing a book was something that wasn't entirely out of my grasp, and as well as being a wonderful source of inspiration, you're also a wonderful friend. Okay, so you never ever stop working (I'm pretty sure your eighth book is sitting next to my first) and you're truly batshit, but I absolutely adore you with all of my heart. You have been through so much, more than many know, and yet your unrelenting smile still lights up every room you walk into. Although this entire book was written around self-acceptance – if I could be more like any other human in the world, I would choose you. I love you.

To Luke Cutforth – my dearest Luke. We have been through so much, both together and apart. So much has changed both between us and all around us since I first made a fan video mentioning you in 2012. We have made each other's dreams come true. If it wasn't for you telling me to take my love of music seriously in 2013, I absolutely would not be where I am today. I would not have released five EPs in five years, I would not have toured arenas with Busted, and I wouldn't have headlined Shepherd's Bush Empire – and you've been there at every tour supporting me. You were there when I shaved all of my hair off, you were there when I fell out with friends and family, you were there through my nagging and shouting, and continue to be there for me whenever I need you. I will be there for you for as long as you need me, watching you chase your own dreams as you did for me. Thank you for changing my life for the better.

To Gerard Groves, Arthur Walwin, Cherry Wallis, Felix

Kjellberg, Marzia Bisognin, PJ Ligouri, Sophie Newton, Jon Barker, Tessa Violet, Dodie Clark, Zoe Sugg and Alfie Deyes – I am so grateful to have you as friends I can count on when I have a problem. Please know that I am there for you too, any time you need me. I spent many years of my life feeling as though I had no friends – you are all the reason I no longer feel that way. Thank you.

To the YouTube creators that first inspired me to put my heart and soul into making videos – Daniel Howell, Phil Lester, Charlie McDonnell, Carrie Hope Fletcher, Ray William Johnson, Shane Dawson and Smosh – you indirectly changed my entire life. Thank you for daring to put your life out there when YouTube was uncharted territory, and thank you for inspiring so many others to do the same. I would not be here if it wasn't for all of you.

Of course, to my subscribers – I'm sorry that I never gave us a cool clique name. Nothing ever sounds good. The Blackberries? The . . . Feel Gooders? We trialled The Fighters once, and I definitely think that fits us the most. When I was younger and going through most of the hardships in this book, I felt as though I didn't have anyone I could talk to that wasn't under the age of forty. If I have ever made you feel less alone in your battles, then everything I do is worth it. Thank you for always being there, whether you've been with me for five days or five years – my life is only the joy it is now because of your unwavering support. Thank you for reading my book. I truly hope with all of my heart that you enjoyed it.

And last but not least . . . to my younger self. We went through some shit, man. We cried a lot, got called a lot of names and often felt weak and alone. Thank you for sticking with the course, refusing to give up entirely and allowing me to blossom from you. I know that I am a completely different person in an entirely different place to what you imagined for me at this stage in my life, but we're doing good, kid. We're happy. We have friends. We feel good.

And we wrote a book!

Endpaper photo credits

Left-hand page:

Middle, right – Emma and her father on stage at Summer in the City after shaving her head for charity, 2014, by LBPhoto.UK

Middle, left – Emma on stage in Dublin for the Busted tour, 2016, by Jane Greenwood

Bottom, centre – Emma on stage at Shepherd's Bush Empire, Magnetised Tour, 2017, by Mark Walker

All other photos from Emma Blackery's personal collection